ALSO BY STACY JOHNSON
Money Made Simple

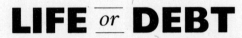

LIFE

or

DEBT

*A One-Week Plan for a
Lifetime of Financial Freedom*

Stacy Johnson

BALLANTINE BOOKS

NEW YORK

*This book is dedicated to two people
who sent me off into the world with the greatest possible gifts:
the belief that I was capable of accomplishing anything
I set my mind to and the ability to laugh at myself.
They are my parents, Stacy and Betty Johnson.*

2005 Ballantine Books Trade Paperback Edition

Copyright © 2002 by Stacy Johnson

Originally published in hardcover in the United States by Ballantine Books, an imprint of The Random House Publishing Group, a division of Random House, Inc., in 2002.

Library of Congress Cataloging-in-Publication Data

Johnson, Stacy.
Life or debt : a one-week plan for a lifetime of financial freedom / Stacy Johnson.
p. cm.
1. Finance, Personal. I. Title.
HG179 .J567 2002
332.024—dc21
2001051287

ISBN 0-345-45564-9

Printed in the United States of America

www.ballantinebooks.com

2 4 6 8 9 7 5 3 1

Text design by Mary A. Wirth

THANKS!

While it's true that we come into this world alone and leave it alone, practically everything else we do of any significance involves the assistance, cooperation, and/or indulgence of other people. That's certainly true of this book. Much of what went into *Life or Debt* came from my own thoughts and observations, but often I confirmed those thoughts by talking to people who were experts at this stuff. That includes many people who work for a debt counseling organization called Consumer Credit Counseling Service. I'll name just a few: Bill Potter in Tampa, Eileen Muhlig in Syracuse, Debbie Harper in Birmingham, and Mary Hulbert in Cincinnati. There were many others.

I also learned a lot from reading other books. One I quote directly and acknowledge in *Life or Debt*, which is *The Millionaire Next Door*. But there are many other books that directly or indirectly influenced me in less specific ways. One I'd like to both

Thanks

mention and recommend that you read is *Your Money or Your Life* by Joe Dominguez and Vicki Robin.

Although I went to college and have earned money and even received awards for writing, that doesn't mean I know the first thing about spelling, grammar, and punctuation. (Proof: While writing that sentence, I actually misspelled the word *grammar*.) But fortunately, I was blessed with a partner who knows all that stuff and more. And she's gorgeous to boot! So thanks to my flawless bride, Gina Maria Germani, for being my editor and inspiration.

CONTENTS

Are You Free?

Are you free? Can you do whatever you want? "Of course!" you might respond. After all, as a nation we've fought wars to guarantee our personal freedoms. Americans are free to do whatever we want, whenever we want, as long as we're not stepping on somebody else when we do it. But hold on a minute. That's just theoretical. There's a big, ugly problem with this supposed freedom we all share. Namely, while we may have the right to do what we want, do we have the ability to do what we want? Do you have the ability to quit your job today and become self-employed? To retire early and travel the world? Will you have the ability to send your kids to the best schools? Are you making a positive impact in the world by offering time and money to the people and causes that deserve it? You may have life and liberty, but do you really have the ability to pursue happiness?

The sad truth is that most of us will admit we don't have the ability to find happiness. Why? Because we're way too busy paying the bills to be free to pursue it. And what a bummer! Because we pass through this life only once: Time is the currency that, once spent, can never be replaced. Of course, you already know that. So let me ask you something. Since your time is limited, why aren't you spending it in a way that makes you the happiest?

You'll probably be able to answer that question in one word: money. Sure, our government says we've got the right to live our lives any way we choose, but what difference does that make if we don't have the resources to do it? And if you can't do what you want, how can you really be free? You can't. And you know what I think? I think that not only can you be free, you owe it to yourself and to your family to become that way. And it's within your reach!

So how do you become free? Your immediate response is probably to say, "Make more money, of course!" But more money isn't the path to freedom. In the song "Me and Bobby McGee," Janis Joplin says, "Freedom is just another word for nothing left to lose." And you know what? While she probably wasn't referring to money, she certainly could have been. Because financial freedom has never been a function of how much money you make. It's always been about how little money you owe. Say you make $50,000 a year and have a $100,000 mortgage and $20,000 of other debts. You might think that if you figured out a way to make $500,000 a year, you'd be "rich." You'd be "free." But odds are, that's not what would happen at all. If you're like most people, you'd soon get a $1 million mortgage to go with your new income, and you'd have $200,000 in other debts. You might appear rich, but it's all just smoke and mirrors. In reality, you're in exactly the same place you started. In fact, you're in an even worse spot. Because climbing higher up the ladder simply provides you with a greater distance to fall. So there you'd be in your giant house with your Porsche in your mortgaged garage, and guess what you'd be thinking? "If I could only make $5 million a year, then I'd be 'rich.' Then I'd be 'free.'"

Introduction

Here's the real deal: There are two kinds of people in the world who can be considered financially free: those who make so much money that they can't possibly spend it all and those who don't owe anybody anything. While very few people find themselves in the first category, almost anybody with a decent income and some determination can find themselves in the second. And when you break free from debt, you can use the same money that you formerly used to make payments to pay for your early retirement instead.

And that is what this book is all about: making you free by removing the shackles of debt, then taking the money you used to use to service all that debt and investing it to make you financially independent. Is it simple? Yes, as you'll soon find out. Is it easy? No, because it requires a new way of thinking, which is never easy to bring about. It also takes time, which for many is an equally difficult concept. But let me tell you, it's worth it. Because since you only get to live once, isn't it better if you spend your life doing what you want to do instead of what you have to do? That's why our journey together is called *Life or Debt*. That's not just a catchy name, it's a choice you make every time you spend money. You'll understand exactly what I mean by that in short order. And by the time you finish reading this book, I promise you'll choose life over debt, and you'll be happy you did.

LIFE *or* DEBT

CHAPTER ONE

My Story

This chapter is about me and my life. It's not necessary for you to know anything about me at all for this plan to work for you, so if you feel like skipping this part of the book, feel free. But I think it may make sense for you to know the person you're getting advice from, so here's the abbreviated version of how I came to be writing *Life or Debt*.

Ever notice how practically all self-help or motivational books start out with the author revealing some sort of catharsis that suddenly caused them to see the light? You know, stuff like "There I was, forty-five years old, living on the street and eating from a Dumpster, when suddenly inspiration struck like a divine lightning bolt! All I had to do was follow the seven magic steps and I'd become rich beyond my wildest expectations. And sure enough, it's happened! Now I have a mansion in Malibu, my own helicopter, and I party at the Playboy mansion." What the author often leaves out, of course, is how much of that newfound wealth comes from following the seven magic steps and how much comes from selling books and videotapes on infomercials and home shopping channels.

Here's the first of many embarrassing admissions I'll make: While I have made my share of stupid mistakes, I've never been poor, gone bankrupt, or had a sudden revelation that laid the "true path" to fame and fortune at my feet. Nor am I rich now, at least not in the "beachhouse in Malibu" sense. And while I hope that I make money from this book (and get invited to the Playboy mansion, for that matter), it's not really that big a deal to me one way or the other. Why? Because my life is fine exactly the way it is. I'm doing precisely what I want to do, and what I make doing it is fine by me.

But that isn't how my life has always been. As you'll soon discover, there was a time—and not so long ago—that I forgot who I was and what I wanted out of life.

Here's how I came to be your humble narrator:

In 1973 I was seventeen years old. For those of you who weren't alive and/or aware at that time, trust me, it was an interesting time to be in America. By 1973, the hippie message of love, peace, and togetherness may have been fading, but you couldn't tell it by talking to me. Another aspect of the love generation that I could especially relate to was the wholesale rejection of all things material. The idea of sharing with your brothers and sisters (that is, everyone younger than thirty) and thereby avoiding the traps that lurked in money, property, and politics seemed both reasonable and realistic. But I wanted to try it for myself. So promptly after graduating from high school, I left my middle-class home in Atlanta and hitchhiked across the country. My goal was to forget how my parents and society had taught me to view the world and instead to live life the way it was meant to be lived: with no obligations and plenty of adventure.

And this wasn't a summer vacation we're talking about here. This was going to be my life. So for several months, that's what I did. I experienced the ultimate in freedom. I went where I wanted, did what I wanted, and stayed as long as I wanted. For most of that time, I didn't have two nickels to rub together. I survived mostly by doing day labor, stuff like furniture delivery or unloading boxcars. Always something different, which was cool because I got to learn how to do lots of things and had the opportunity to meet lots of people. Then, when I'd satisfied my curiosity and earned enough to meet my meager needs, I moved on. My ultimate goal was to reach the Mecca of my generation: San Francisco and Haight-Ashbury. That was the capital of this brave new nation, where society was being reinvented, where free love and flower power were going to replace greed and war. When I pictured my future, I saw myself pitching in at a commune or homesteading in Alaska. Naive? Of course, but hey, this is my story. So stop laughing and listen.

You can probably guess what happened during the course of my personal path to spiritual enlightenment. It didn't take long to figure out that the love and peace movement was either nonexistent or at least so far underground that I couldn't dig it up. What I did find a lot of, however, were deviants, con artists, and common crooks. That's not to say I never found genuine, kind, caring people. I did. But by the time I reached San Francisco, I understood that flower power was an idea whose time had either come and gone or had existed more in song than in real, day-to-day life. I also had firsthand experience that many of the people living on the streets weren't poets and adventurers who had rejected the possession-obsession society; they were people who were rejected by that society and had no place else to go. So while I valued my experiences, I realized that this was not the life I wanted to lead.

After I returned to Atlanta, my life soon began to resemble those of my more traditional contemporaries. I went away to college. And since the freedom of the road hadn't lived up to my lofty expectations, I thought I'd try a more old-fashioned way of finding freedom: making tons of money! My dreams of home-steading in Alaska were gradually replaced with visions of yachts, mansions, and Penthouse Pets. Seem like a major about-face? I guess it was. But considering my newfound cynicism about the hippie movement, and taking into account that virtually every mass-media, peer, and parental message I ever received was all about acquiring money, my transformation was both simple and rapid.

I started college intending to major in philosophy, but by my junior year I decided that accounting would take me where I wanted to go a lot faster. In retrospect, I believe the reason I chose that particular degree went back to a casual dinner conver-sation I'd had with my father years before. I must have been about twelve or thirteen years old. While talking about one of his old friends who was a CPA, he had casually mentioned that CPAs were never out of work and always made a good living. So there you have it! Security, money, and parental approval all rolled into one. In any case, I graduated in 1977 with a degree in accounting, cut my hair, and took a job with the state of Arizona as an auditor.

Unfortunately, there was an integral part of accounting that my dad had forgotten to mention to me at that dinner years be-fore: An accountant has to go to work and actually do accounting for eight hours a day, five days a week. While some people may find this an exciting and rewarding way to occupy their working lives, for me it was like watching paint dry, only slower. Still, an-other thing my dad had taught me was that work wasn't supposed to be fun ("That's why they call it work!"). So I did it for a few years, picking up my CPA certificate along the way and trying to ignore the narcolepsy that had become a prominent feature of my working life.

By 1981, I came to the conclusion that I'd rather chop off my own foot with a dull ax than be an accountant for a minute longer. In other words, my fear of being out of work had finally been outweighed by the despair I was enduring in my chosen profession. Besides, I had another idea that would forward my ambitions to obscene wealth a lot faster. In the office building where I worked, there was a big E. F. Hutton office. And it looked really cool—a giant open space filled with desks and people and a stock ticker dancing across the front of the room. There was even a place for spectators! Can you imagine an office job so interesting that people actually stopped to watch? You could practically feel the excitement just walking by the place. Bye-bye, crummy salary! Bye-bye, narcolepsy! And it went without saying that these guys would hire me. After all, investing in stocks was all about analyzing companies, and who could do that better than a CPA?

I'll never forget my first interview with the manager of E. F. Hutton. He peered at my completed application as though it included a lengthy prison record. This was confusing. After all, I was a CPA—a master of numbers and financial analysis! But when I finally found the courage to verbalize the obvious, his exact words were, "I'd much rather have a used-car salesman sitting across the desk from me right now than a CPA." I was stunned. Potentially doomed by an alarming lack of sales experience!

Fortunately, the news wasn't all bad. Because despite the embarrassingly inappropriate education and professional credentials I was saddled with, I was able to convince my tormentor that I did possess the one personality trait necessary to the success of any stockbroker: I was desperately greedy! He told me that after a few years of hard work (which, as he explained, actually entailed doing nothing more than using the telephone to mercilessly harass sixty or seventy innocent people every day), I could expect to make $50,000 a year, maybe more. And that was just about all the money in the world to me, since I was making only $18,000 at the time. I told him that there was nothing, short of murder, that I wouldn't do to make $50,000. And despite the fact that I had drawn the line at capital crime (probably a mistake in retrospect), he decided that I at least warranted a test to see if I could actually sell. I passed and was subsequently hired, trained, and licensed in stocks, mutual funds, commodities, and life insurance.

In many ways, being a stockbroker was exactly what I had hoped. It was exciting, especially compared with auditing school districts. And my manager hadn't been exaggerating about the money, either, probably because I had stumbled into the stock brokerage business with nearly perfect timing. When I started my career in 1981, the Dow Jones Industrial Average was around 800 and interest rates on risk-free money market accounts were around 15 percent, so pretty much nobody wanted to invest in stocks. But in 1982, rates started to plummet and the stock market began what turned out to be one of the greatest bull markets of the century. This rising tide floated all ships, including mine. Less than three years after being hired, I was indeed making $50,000 a year. As I closed in on my thirtieth birthday, I was working ninety hours a week, and my income had grown to more than $100,000 a year. Not exactly rich, but I was certainly a success, especially when I compared myself to my parents and the friends I'd grown up with. Like many people who find themselves making big money, I honestly believed that I deserved it. After all, I was making a lot of money for my clients, wasn't I? And I was certainly making a lot of money for my employer. Therefore I must be smart, and therefore deserving, right?

So since my hitchhiking days of all freedom and no money, the pendulum had swung to the other extreme. The 1960s are known historically as the "love generation," and the 1980s are often called the "greed generation." For me, at least, both labels fit like a glove. The altruism and idealism of the 1960s became distant memories as the 1980s marched on and my income continued to rise.

Now I was making money, which I had exchanged for free

time. But that was cool, because I enjoyed my job. In fact, let's be honest: I didn't just enjoy my job, I *was* my job. And my job was money. I made it, I borrowed it, I invested it, and I blew it. Just as I had in my hitchhiking youth, I took my cue from my peers, only this time the message was different. If you've got it, flaunt it! You can't take it with you! So I bought the big house with a pool, a few convertibles, and some rental property, and of course I did a lot of investing and outright gambling in the stock market. I had debt, but it was a small fraction of my income, so it didn't matter. What did matter was that I was a big deal, and nobody would know it if I didn't look like one, act like one, dress like one, travel like one, and party like one.

I haven't been a stockbroker now for more than ten years, so I can't say what happens in that business these days. But I can tell you what it was like in the 1980s, and in many ways the picture isn't pretty. Stockbrokers were measured almost entirely by how much money they made for themselves and for the company. Money made for customers was incidental. Of course, the management of these companies would surely take exception to that remark, probably bleating something like "That's a lie! Our clients are important. If we don't make money for them, we won't keep them, and therefore we are compelled to do right by them." While that argument may be logical, the fact remains that where I worked, every morning the previous day's commission tally was displayed on a clipboard outside the manager's office so you could see not only how much you had made, but how much everyone else had made as well. Client profits, losses, and satisfaction were never displayed. Brokers generating the most commissions got the biggest offices, were held up as examples at sales meetings, and were sent on luxury cruises. Those who didn't generate much in the way of commissions, regardless of what they did for their clients, were relegated to the small cubicles that made up the "bullpen" and in many cases were ultimately fired. To my knowledge, nobody was ever retained for treating customers well. At the same time, brokers whom I absolutely, positively knew to be unethical were being heaped with recognition. While the argument that treating customers well is necessary to survive may sound logical, the truth is that replacing the customer was easier than replacing their poorly invested money. That's not to say that brokers, even unethical ones, would deliberately hurt people; after all, the more money your customer makes, the more you have to manage. But salespeople are by nature competitive, and recognition in the investment game is about commissions, not client profits. Of course, I didn't see that back then, at least not for the first few years. It took a long time, and some painful experiences, for me to learn this simple lesson.

In 1985 I got married. I met my wife on an airplane coming back from a sales meeting, and it was immediately apparent that we had two major things in common. First, I really felt the need to display a great-looking, sexy girl, and she was one. Second, she really felt the need to spend money, and I had some. Perfect match! My close friends tried to point out that that might not be enough for a lasting relationship, but what did they know?

As it turned out, they were frustratingly correct. (Don't you hate when that happens?) In 1987, after little more than a year of a lot less than marital bliss, I was separated from both my wife and a major amount of cash. In the meantime, as a little salt in the wound, on October 19 of that year the stock market crashed. Down 23 percent in one day! Talk about scary. About the only good thing that happened to me in 1987 was that I expanded into TV broadcasting. I was invited to do ongoing investment commentary during the morning news on a local television station, probably due to interest surrounding the stock market after Black Monday. It was a nonpaying job at first, but one that enhanced my visibility and credibility in the community, always a good thing for any salesman.

For a while things went pretty well. I was single again and by

1990 had met the woman who was the real deal. Also in 1990, my success as a stockbroker and visibility on the news helped land me a job managing the local office of another major brokerage firm. I had met the right girl, I was a genuine vice president, and my earnings were now in excess of $200,000 a year. More important, I had also started maturing when it came to money and when it came to ethics.

About the time that I became a manager, I had finally begun to realize that showing off by driving the fanciest car and living in the fanciest house wasn't all that important. In retrospect, perhaps I had an intuition that it was time to start preparing myself for a new life. Maybe it was because my subconscious was telling me that the inevitable collision between my personal ethics and the brokerage business was about to cut short my career. Maybe it was my conscious mind that told me that taking care of all this stuff I had collected was stressing me out and making me miserable. Looking back, I honestly don't know what changed me. But I do know that instead of expanding my lifestyle, I started selling stuff and using my money to pay off debts and build up savings.

As to ethics, after ten or so years as a stockbroker, I was beginning to have a hard time looking at myself in the mirror. It wasn't because I had ripped people off. Even at my greediest, I had always acted in a way that I honestly believed to be in my clients' best interests. Of course, the stock market itself, along with the stupid investment products pushed by the firms I worked for, had often overcome my good intentions, but I had done my best. The problem was that it was becoming increasingly apparent that the financial services industry stank to high heaven. I won't go into more specifics than I already have; this is my story, not theirs, and besides, that's a whole book by itself. Suffice it to say that a simple fact that should always have been obvious to me now became unavoidable: This business cares a lot more for its own bottom line than it does for its clients'. I was really starting to feel unable to carry on. My own greed, along with a healthy dose of ignorance, had allowed me to be blind to that problem more often than not for years, but it just wasn't enough anymore. I was rapidly approaching the same misery level I had achieved as an accountant.

So here I was at a real turning point in my life. I felt it was time to close this door. What door was I going to open next?

I took my time, and thought long and hard about what I had done up to then with my life, trying to see the big picture. I had started with the idealism typical of youth, then abruptly gone the opposite way and focused only on myself and my needs. It was high time to find a balance I could live with.

What I decided to do was start over, only this time to do it the right way. The "right" way is a choice as unique as each of us, but for me it was to do something that I enjoyed that was also worthwhile. Something that I could feel good about, have fun at, and still get paid for. Which for me meant doing TV. I loved telling the truth about money to people who appreciated hearing it, rather than forcing some financial product down the throats of unsuspecting people trying to eat dinner. And since giving good, honest advice obviously has value, sooner or later someone would write me a check for it. Plus, I was imminently qualified, having collected a slew of credentials and spent my entire adult life in the business of money.

At the age of thirty-five, I started my life over. I married the perfect woman, and I went out and started selling television stations my very own news product: _Money Talks_. I could take this risk because I had reined in my spending, pretty much paid off my debts, and, despite my ex-wife's best efforts, still had a few dollars left. Ten years later, I'm still doing TV. I'm on the air in more than eighty cities. I tell the truth, and while I don't make the money I once did, I'm a much happier person.

It's too early to tell whether you're going to get anything valuable from this book. But I can promise you this: You wouldn't be reading it in the first place if I had quit my job with lots of debt and no savings. Fact is, if I hadn't started marching to my own drummer and instead had continued to follow my peers by living up to my spending and borrowing capacity, I wouldn't have had the time or the money even to think about what my destiny was, much less move toward it. And while I hope that you're never forced by conscience or circumstance to start over, as I was, I do hope that you'll have the ability to. Maybe you've got something valuable to say, something that I and a million other people really need to hear. I can't stand the thought of your being so consumed by supporting an unrewarding lifestyle that you don't have the freedom to sit down and tell it to us. And that, gentle reader, is what this book is all about.

So that's been my journey thus far. Here are a few thoughts that summarize some of the lessons that I've learned along the way.

The first I expressed above: that the simple choices about borrowing and spending that you're making right now can have a far-reaching impact, not just on your life, but on the lives of those around you and beyond. Living without debt makes it much more likely that you'll have the freedom to fulfill your destiny.

Lesson number two: There's nothing wrong with *being* your job, provided your job reflects who you really are. If it doesn't, then if you're lucky, you'll fail. If you're unlucky, you'll succeed and as a result quite possibly waste your life doing something that isn't you. You'll be miserable, and there's no amount of money that will take that misery away.

Lesson number three: Money buys things, not happiness. And each thing you have comes with its own invisible ball and chain. Attach enough of them to your life, and you'll feel like a prisoner, because that's exactly what you'll be.

Lesson number four: Every person or company you owe money to owns you. Why? Because they have a say in the most intimate details of your life. When (or if) you retire. Where (or if) your kids go to college. How you use (or if you ever have any) leisure time. Buying and borrowing forces you to use your time to earn money. And working, especially in an unrewarding job, could separate you from your destiny and from happiness.

In a way, my life has been circular. My teenage visions of a world of peace, love, sharing, and caring may have been naive, but as I reflect back, they were much closer to my version of true happiness than the greed and possession-obsession that symbolized the first part of my adult life. Today I've found a happy medium. I don't sleep in underpasses and forsake all things material. But I also don't squander my precious time or personal integrity so that I can resemble people in TV commercials or receive accolades from people who don't matter. I do what makes me happy, and I stay as free as possible by not owing my time to anyone.

Wanna join me? It's easier than you think!

CHAPTER TWO

Who Wants to Be a Millionaire?

Maybe instead of sitting in front of the boob tube watching people take their shot at fame and fortune with Regis, you'd rather play a personal home version of becoming a millionaire. Well, the home version takes a lot longer than half an hour to play, but the good news is that you won't have to know the answers to trivial questions, and your odds of winning are a lot higher. Plus, there aren't any commercials to sit through!

An old friend of mine (we'll call him Art, because that's his name) financed his way through college with a wrestling scholarship. While Art was obviously a good wrestler, he wasn't Olympic quality, and he was wise enough to see that early on. So one day he requested a private audience with the coach. He asked, "What can I do to be a better wrestler? Should I try a different diet? More running? More weight lifting? I'll do anything . . . just tell me." And what the coach said was this:

"You know who the winners are on our team, right?"

Art said, "Of course."

The coach said, "Then hang around with them. Become friends with them. In short, just watch the winners and do what they do."

Art still never wrestled in the Olympics, but when he followed this advice his performance improved dramatically, as did his ability to wrestle with every other problem life has since placed in his path.

Isn't that great advice? If you want your life to resemble some-one else's in some way, then simply watch that person and do what he or she does. If what you want is to be financially independent, it makes sense to see what millionaires did to get that way. And you don't have to risk a stalking conviction to do it, because there are plenty of sources for that information.

When I was a stockbroker, I dealt with lots of people who had a million dollars in net worth. Here's what I learned. Becoming wealthy has almost nothing to do with income or investment know-how. Accumulating wealth comes from avoiding debt, living below your means, and investing sensibly and consistently. Among the hundreds of people I served during my years as a stockbroker, with the exception of those who inherited, nearly every wealthy person I met got that way by following this simple path. Conversely, among my myriad clients who gambled on options, commodities, penny stocks, sophisticated trading strategies, or other get-rich-quick schemes, not a single one was a long-term winner. Las Vegas offers better odds, and the drinks are free.

Of course, it would be much more exciting if the path to wealth were a dramatic half-hour quiz show. Or if it involved lay-ing down a big bet on getrich.com stock or buying a lottery ticket. But go out seeking real, live millionaires, and what you'll probably find is that a vast majority of them are so mundane in appearance, attitude, and occupation that they virtually blend into the background. By and large, they don't wear flashy suits, drive fancy cars, wear a Rolex, or live in a big house. Why should they? They don't need to impress anyone. If you're looking at someone who's flashy, odds are he sells things to rich people for a living but isn't rich himself.

Have you read *The Millionaire Next Door*? You should. It's a great book, because it proves what I observed about rich people with objective statistics. What authors Thomas Stanley and William Danko did was personally interview five hundred millionaires as well as collect information from another one thousand with a detailed survey. Here are a few of the things they found out:

Income: Median annual income for American millionaires is $131,000.

Cars: Fewer than one in four millionaires own a new car. Fewer than one in five lease. The average price paid for a car is a little less than twenty-five grand. For more than one-third, their most recent purchase was a used car. Only 6.4 percent of millionaires surveyed drive a Mercedes or a Lexus. Less than 3 percent drive a Jag. Nearly 60 percent drive an American car.

Clothes: Of the millionaires surveyed, 50 percent had never paid more than $400 for a suit in their entire lives, for themselves or anyone else. About half had also never paid more than $140 for a pair of shoes.

Houses: Of the millionaires surveyed, 97 percent own their own homes. The average value of that home is $320,000, and about half of the millionaires have lived in that house for twenty years or more.

What's fascinating about this information is that it is so remarkably different from what we think of when we imagine the life of a millionaire. We've been trained to think of millionaires as they're portrayed on *Lifestyles of the Rich and Famous*. But the truth is that an opulent lifestyle isn't at all typical of the average millionaire. Why? The answer is very basic: Very few people can afford to both look wealthy and actually become wealthy during the same lifetime. You have to make a choice as to which you want to do.

Bottom line? What I learned when I was a stockbroker, and what you'll learn when you read books like this or *The Millionaire Next Door*, is that becoming financially independent isn't really a function of how much money you make. It's much more often a function of how little money you spend.

So do you really want to be a millionaire? If so, turn off the quiz show and take the advice of Art's wrestling coach. Watch the winners and simply do what they do. And yes, Regis, that's my final answer!

CHAPTER THREE

Life or Debt

This book is designed to get you completely out of debt as quickly as possible. And once you're out from under those payments, the money that used to go to service all that debt is going to make you financially free. Free to do anything and everything you always wanted to do. Free to retire without help from the government, your relatives, or any other source of income. Or maybe just free to stop banging your head against the wall at a job you hate.

My wife, Gina, spent most of her working life in journalism, first in print, later as a television news reporter, and finally as a primary news anchor for a TV station in Cincinnati. About a year and a half ago, she quit. Maybe you can relate to the reason she quit: She just couldn't stomach her job anymore. In her case, she felt that the quality of TV news had gotten so bad that just turning out a journalistically sound newscast was becoming a nightly battle. In other words, she felt the standards in her industry weren't up to her personal standards. (Perhaps that's a thought you can also relate to your job.) Gina made a choice: to leave the job and the money behind. It was a tough decision, but at least money didn't enter into it much. She had the freedom to choose a new path because we didn't need her income. Why? Because we've always chosen to live "beneath our means." Most households don't have the freedom to make choices like that, because most owe for as much car, house, vacation, and lifestyle as two incomes can buy. Which means that right now, all across America, there are people who are suffering because they're forced to do something they don't feel right about doing. I hope you're not one of those people, but if you are, you won't be for long. Because you're going to have the freedom that financial independence buys.

As I said in the introduction to this book, finding financial independence is simple, but it's not easy. Simple, because the steps are straightforward. But not easy, because to succeed it's likely that you're going to have to fundamentally change the habits of a lifetime. So if we don't talk for a while about how you got into debt in the first place, it's not likely that you'll complete the steps to become debt-free. And even if you do, it's not likely that you'll stay that way.

If you find yourself chained to debt, the first thing you should realize is that you're not alone. Not by a long shot. There's more than a trillion dollars of personal debt in the United States right now, and about a third of it is credit card debt. Know how much that is? We're so desensitized to numbers like "billion" and even "trillion" these days, maybe that doesn't mean much. But consider this: If you stacked hundred-dollar bills on top of one another, a million dollars would be about six feet high. A billion dollars, though, would be more than a mile high! So just the credit card debt in this country would translate into a stack of hundreds reaching more than 350 miles high—a debt that's truly out of this world! And that giant tower of debt is sucking the independence out of your life and gradually transforming it into corporate profits.

Another thing you should realize about debt—if you have it, you're right where you're supposed to be. Or, more accurately, you're right where "they" want you to be. Who is this evil "they" that wants to enslave you? You'll see. But first, let's take a look at where we Americans find ourselves today.

Most Americans retire dependent on government, church, or family assistance. Most depend on Social Security for the majority of their retirement income. Most work until they reach retirement age. Most enter their retirement years with very little in the bank. And most American adults use credit. (Hmmm. Wonder if there could be a relationship among these things?) I could drone on and on with more facts and figures, but I'm not going to because they really don't matter anyway. What matters is how much money you make and how much of it you manage to hold on to.

What's nuts about so many of us retiring poor is that it's not necessary. Why? Because most of us will earn more than $1 million during our lifetimes. (Don't think so? Even an income of just $25,000 per year multiplied by 40 working years is $1 million!) Granted, we obviously have to use a lot of the money we make to survive. Still, it seems that many of us make *mucho* during our working lives, yet nearly all of us seem to end up with *nada*. What's going on here?

Well, one thing that's going on here is that you're surrendering a lot of your money to your rich uncle in Washington, D.C. I'm speaking, of course, of Uncle Sam. But unless you're ready to collect some guns and move to Montana, there's probably not much you can do about that. (There actually are some little things you can do to reduce your taxes. But for the most part, taxes are like in-laws: we may not like 'em, but they're a part of the package.)

But another, bigger thing is happening to you every day to separate you from your freedom. And this one you do have control over. Namely, you can stop paying three times more for the stuff you buy than it should cost.

What the heck do I mean by that? Well, let's say you buy a $100,000 house with no money down and pay for it with a thirty-year mortgage loan. Let's say the interest rate on your mortgage is 9.4 percent. Your monthly payments will be $833. (That's just for the principal and interest and doesn't include all the other stuff you'll have to pay, like mortgage insurance, homeowners insurance, and real estate taxes.) By the time you've paid for that house, you will have paid $200,000 in interest! So you've actually paid $300,000 for your house, not $100,000. And Uncle Sam makes it worse. Assuming you're in a 30 percent tax bracket, you might have to earn up to $400,000 to have $300,000 after taxes to pay that additional $200,000 of interest on your $100,000 house. That means you have to work like a slave for decades to earn $400,000 to buy your house. And half of that money, $200,000, went for the sole purpose of fattening some lender's profit margin.

What about that nice vacation you just took to the Bahamas? Or that stereo you bought? Or those clothes you absolutely had to have? Well, if you used plastic and time payments to buy them, you could again be paying three times more than they cost.

Let's say the total of all this stuff you charged to your Visa card amounted to $5,000. Your interest rate is 17 percent, and you have to pay a minimum of 2 percent of the balance every month or $10, whichever is greater. (Those are pretty common terms in credit card land.) Now, while you show off that Caribbean tan, rock to that radical stereo, and go stylin' in those new threads, you're making minimum payments on your Visa bill. Here's what will happen:

First of all, if you never use that plastic again, you'll still be making payments for a little more than forty years. And when it's over, you'll have paid a total of $16,304: $5,000 for the stuff you bought and $11,304 in interest. Bottom line? Again, you've paid three times what the stuff costs. And again, because of taxes, you might have to earn $23,291 to pay $16,304 for stuff that you thought you paid $5,000 for. And just to rub a little salt in the wound, do you think you'll still have that tan, that stereo, or those awesome threads forty years from now?

These numbers are eye-popping enough standing alone. But when you compare it to what you could have been doing with that same money during that same time period, you're really going to start understanding why so many people retire with nothing. More important, you're going to start getting a grip on why your own freedom has been right there next to you the whole time.

Suppose you'd paid cash for that $100,000 house of yours. (I know that's a stretch, but work with me here.) And suppose that instead of paying $833 every month, you were investing $833 every month. And suppose that instead of paying 9.4 percent interest, you were earning 9.4 percent interest. Result? After thirty years, you'd have $1,658,222! Of course, if you'd paid 30 percent in taxes every year along the way, you'd have "only" $935,902.

Okay, let's take a break from the numbers for a second, sit back and consider what we've discovered. Number one: When we borrow to buy things, we're really taking on a third job. Our first job is where we go every morning to collect a paycheck. Our second job is working for our government, since we're giving a major chunk of our money to them. Our third job is padding the pockets of the giant companies that are in the business of lending us money. Working for your boss and the government is bad enough. But do you really need to go to work for Visa, too? I don't have the time!

That leads us to the second thing we've learned—that compound interest is a fabulous tool. When we borrow money, we're using it to make major money for other people. But when we harness the miracle of compound interest by saving and investing our money, we're using that same powerful tool to build financial freedom for ourselves.

The trick is to stop being a blind, obedient, hardworking slave to debt and start redirecting your money so it works like a slave for you. End result? Freedom, baby!

Now, maybe you're saying, "Okay, okay! I see how interest is costing me big bucks, and I'll try to keep it to a minimum. Will you get off my back already?" Sorry, not yet. Because even if you never borrow a dime, you're still sacrificing your financial freedom every time you spend money anyway. Let's talk about that next.

In fact, let's do a simple exercise together. Let's take a minute and glance around our respective rooms. (If you're not at home right now, imagine that you are.) Notice all the stuff in the room you're sitting in, and I'll do the same. Now, let's take one or two of these things and see what they're really costing us. Ready? I'll start. I'm sitting on a leather chair that cost $1,000. My wife bought it for me for my birthday. I know that's a lot for a chair, but it's really cool, and besides, I spend a lot of time here. (See how I'm justifying myself? And I don't even know you!) Anyway, if my chair was bought with credit, and paid for over time with minimum payments, how much did it cost? If you've been paying attention, you know that it could have cost up to $3,000: $1,000 for the chair and $2,000 for the credit card company. Happily, however, that isn't the case with my chair. (As you might imagine, we're not heavily into credit and here.) But it still cost me a lot more than $1,000. Because the money is no longer around to work for me. If it was, and I had invested it and earned 10 percent every year, twenty years from now have $6,727 instead of a worn-out chair.

My chair good example because it cost a nice round number, one that you can use to help you do this same exercise in your home. In other words, if you paid $10 for some item in your room, multiply that $10 by 6.7, and you'll know how much you would have had if you had invested that $10 at 10 percent for twenty years. So your $10 ashtray costs you $67. And that $3 pack of cigarettes you're filling it with costs you about $20.

What I'm describing here is a term that you might want to become acquainted with: "opportunity cost." It simply describes what money you spend today *costs* you in terms of the *opportunity* to have more money tomorrow. And that cost isn't measured just in money. It's measured in something a lot more precious: time.

Let's go back to my chair. We've discovered that the opportunity cost of my chair is $6,727. You know how long I could live on $6,727? Two months easy, maybe three. So, ignoring inflation, I theoretically could have retired at least two months earlier if I weren't sitting in a $1,000 chair right now. What I have chosen to do is swap at least two months of total financial freedom in the future for a nice chair today. Was that a good trade-off?

Of course, I have to sit somewhere while I'm writing this, don't I? But wouldn't I have been better off buying this chair at a garage sale for $100 instead of owning it new for $1,000? A $100 chair would have a twenty-year opportunity cost of $670. So I'd still be retiring $670 later than if I'd sat on the floor working for twenty years. But retiring $670 later instead of sitting on the floor for twenty years is a swap I can live with.

Another way of measuring opportunity cost is comparing the stuff you've bought to how much you make an hour when you work. Let's say you work forty hours a week, fifty weeks a year, and make an annual $40,000 salary. That comes out to exactly $20 an hour. But hold on. You don't actually bring home that much, do you? Nope. You've got to pay taxes on that money. If you're paying 30 percent in taxes, you're actually making $14 an hour. So if you're sitting in a $1,000 chair like mine right now, you were apparently willing to work an extra 480 hours over the next twenty years to do it ($6,720 divided by $14 equals 480). Think how many hours that is. That's twelve weeks—three months! When was the last time you took three months off?

Suppose I came to you and said, "Here's a $1,000 chair. It's yours. All you have to do is work for me without pay for three months." Is that a deal you'd jump at? Doubtful. Yet that's exactly what you're doing every time you spend $1,000, even if you aren't borrowing a penny to do it.

By the way, if you're making $20 an hour, you're probably making even less than $14 in reality. Because in addition to taxes, all kinds of other costs are associated with showing up to get that $14 every hour. You've probably got to drive to where you work, which costs you money. And unless you work at a nudist camp, you've also got to show up with suitable clothes on, clothes that you might have to pay to have dry-cleaned. You might be eating out for lunch, which obviously costs more than if you were eating at home. And if your job stresses you out because it's not providing you with fulfillment, you probably also spend money doing things to alleviate that stress, like having the occasional cocktail or two at after-work "bitch sessions" with your buddies. Or taking vacations or indulging in other leisure activities that reflect what you really like doing. It all adds up, and when you take the time to calculate what you're going to find is that you're making a lot less money than you thought and you're using way too much of your precious time to do it.

So here's the next exercise I want you to do. Unless you're smarter than I am (a distinct possibility), you're probably going to need a calculator to do this, so have one handy before you start.

1. *Write down your annual salary* or, if you're hourly, about how much money you make every year. _____

2. *Multiply the number above by .7 (to account for taxes) and write the answer here.* _____ (Special note to those who are sticklers for detail: I realize that our tax system is incremental. In other words, if you're in a 30 percent tax bracket, not all of your income is taxed at 30 percent, only the part that exceeds established boundaries. But it's also true that federal income tax is the tip of the iceberg. You pay 6.2 percent of your income in Social Security tax. You pay 1.45 percent in Medicare tax. You pay up to 6.2 percent in federal unemployment on the first $7,000 you make. Depending on where you live, you may also be paying state and local income taxes, as well as state unemployment and workers' compensation. So all in all, I'm perfectly comfortable with this 30 percent figure.)

3. *Take a few minutes to think about all the expenses that are associated with your job* every year (gas, food, clothing, and so on). When you've got a rough idea, subtract that number from the answer you got in number 2 and write that amount here. _____

4. *Divide the number above by 2,000* (the number of hours the average person gets paid to work every year) and write that answer here. _____ This is your *true hourly wage*.

What you now have in front of you is how much you're *really* making every time you trade an hour of your life for that paycheck. Depressed? Well, grab a hankie, because it's about to get a lot worse.

5. Now take a few minutes off while you look around your house. *Estimate the price of all the useless "stuff" you've accumulated over the years.* I'm talking about stuff you thought you wanted at the time but in fact don't really use that often, as opposed to the things you really like or really need. When you get a rough estimate, write that amount here. _____

6. Take the amount in number 5 above and multiply it by 6.7 to calculate its twenty-year opportunity cost. Write that answer here. _____

7. Divide the answer from number 6 above by your "true" hourly wage. (It's the number from 4.) Write that answer here. _____

If you actually went through this exercise, what you've just uncovered is the number of hours of slave labor, hours you can never replace, that went into surrounding yourself with this "stuff" you didn't really want or need. And keep in mind that this is if you paid cash for everything. If you used credit, the final tally is obviously much worse. Feel like going to the mall?

By the way, if you didn't actually take the time to do this exercise, then you can add whatever you paid for this book to the list of "stuff" you didn't really want or need.

A word about inflation. Inflation, which refers to the erosion of the purchasing power of money, is a normal part of any healthy economy, and can radically affect the buying power of any money you accumulate over a long period of time. In other words, because the price of stuff tends to go up over time, the value of money today is greater than the value of money tomorrow, and much greater than the value of money twenty or thirty years from now. Let's consider the house example I used before. I said that if you invested $833 every month and earned 9.4 percent, in thirty years you'd end up with $1,658,222. That's true, but if the price of everything went up 3 percent every year during that thirty-year period, you'd be able to buy only the same stuff that $683,165 would buy today. In other words, having $1.6 million in the bank thirty years from now would be like having about seven hundred grand in the bank now. Of course, there's nothing wrong with having seven hundred grand in the bank; it's still a lot of money. But it's only fair to point out all the math, not just the math that makes my message more appealing. After all, this isn't an infomercial.

So inflation could have a serious impact on the money you'll accumulate using any savings plan, including the one I'll be describing here. Still, there's also good news when it comes to inflation: First, not everything goes up in price over time, and second, you're more in control of your own personal inflation than you might think.

What goes down in price over time? Lots of stuff. Priced a VCR lately? A computer? Long distance? Airline tickets? Improvements in technology tend to make some household goods and services cheaper over time rather than more expensive.

More important is that just because you see an annual inflation rate of 3 percent doesn't mean that everything in your life has gone up by 3 percent, or that the purchasing power of your savings has declined that much. Because you have a lot of control over how you spend at least a large portion of your money, that means you have control over just how much inflation you experience in your life. When you hear on the news that inflation was 3 percent last year, what you're probably hearing is that the Consumer Price Index, measured monthly by the government, went up by 3 percent last year. And what is the government measuring to come up with that number? They're measuring the prices of 80,000 different consumer goods and services in 200 categories. These categories can be summarized in eight groups: Food and Beverage, Housing, Clothing, Transportation, Medical Care, Recreation, Education and Communication, and the ever-popular Other category. But if you're not buying stuff that's going up, then you're not experiencing inflation. For example, the food and beverage category includes breakfast cereal, milk, coffee, chicken, wine, full-service meals, and snacks. If you eat an apple from your own tree for breakfast and don't eat out much, your food inflation rate is going to be lower than that of people who eat out a lot and eat breakfast cereal. Clothing includes men's shirts and sweaters, women's dresses, and jewelry. If you buy yours used or not at all that year, again, you're not affected. Housing includes rent: Hopefully you won't be paying any. Recreation includes televisions, cable television, pets and pet products, sports equipment, and admissions to amusement parks and such. This will affect some people in a major way, others not at all.

See where I'm going here? I'm not saying inflation doesn't exist, and as such we have to acknowledge it. But at the same time, 1.6 million dollars in savings is worth only seven hundred grand to those people who are purchasing a basket of 80,000 new products at the store every year. So while your personal inflation rate could be more than 3 percent, odds are that if you follow this program, it will be a lot less.

Before we start getting into the guts of just how we're going to put together your program to get totally out of debt and start saving serious bucks, I want to talk about one more thing: How did we get here? I mean, I hope the numbers I showed you earlier were a pretty compelling reason to stop spending and borrowing and to start saving. Or to put it another way, to stop trading your life for someone else's profit. But these numbers are no mystery, and I didn't just discover them. In fact, you may well have already seen something resembling this logic before. So if all that's common knowledge, why do so many people apparently ignore it?

To make a long story short, you were brainwashed. Somewhere along the line, as a society we've come to believe that, like spoiled children, we deserve to have what we want, when we want it, whether or not we have the money at the time to pay for it. A hundred years ago, there was no such thing. By and large, you bought the things you could afford to pay cash for and did without the things you couldn't pay cash for. It wasn't that there weren't moneylenders around back then. If you've ever read the Bible, you know that moneylenders have been around for thousands of years. So what changed? Our attitude toward borrowing. And why did that change? Largely because lots of companies were willing to spend tons of money to change it. Why were they willing to spend all that money? To make money for themselves. And how did they turn us all into the spoiled brats we are today? That part is simple enough: They used advertising to change our thought process. They got us to stop focusing on price and focus on payments instead. So instead of a car costing $25,000, suddenly it costs $300 a month. A house no longer costs $100,000, it costs $833 a month. A stereo isn't $1,000, it's $30 a month. And as long as we can afford the payments, why shouldn't we have the things we "want" right now? They also used advertising to convince us that owning and displaying a bunch of physical objects would enhance our sex appeal and self-worth. Of course, these companies couldn't have done this to us without our help. They led us to this candy store, but we were more than willing to stuff our faces.

A viewer recently sent me an e-mail that I'd regard as typical. Essentially, this woman is drowning in debt and is looking for a way out. She's not looking to improve her financial life, she's fighting to save it. She and her husband make a little more than $50,000 a year combined and are saddled with a credit card debt of more than $30,000. She'd tried credit counseling but felt the advice was useless, since it involved reducing their expenses, and she felt their expenses were already at an absolute minimum. Here's a direct quote from her e-mail: "The only expenses we have are fixed. We very rarely eat out, and when we do, we share plates. We don't go to the movies or even rent them. I take my lunch to work, my husband has to buy his occasionally because he is a salesman. We cut out all the 'extras' on our phones except for call waiting . . . we have basic cable . . . etc."

When I read this e-mail, I literally laughed out loud. Here's a person who's teetering on the brink of financial disaster and look at the examples she gives to illustrate her frugality: "We cut out all the 'extras' on our phone, except for call waiting . . . we have basic cable . . . etc." These are necessities? If I were two steps from bankruptcy court, I doubt very much that I'd regard basic cable and call waiting as necessities. I probably would also choose not to eat out at all, at least until I had a spending plan in place and my debt under control. Where are these people's heads at? Despite the fact that billions of people in the world live without these things, this couple is apparently convinced that call waiting and cable are as important as oxygen. And this e-mail is hardly exceptional. I've received dozens of similar ones over the last ten years. Don't get me wrong: I'm not saying cable is bad, or call waiting, for that matter. I'm merely pointing out how twisted our minds have become as a result of advertising.

Our willingness to trade our lives for things we don't really want or need comes as a direct result of moneylenders and other advertisers pandering to basic human nature.

When talking about our human nature, it's important to recognize the major role that fear plays in our lives. Not the perfectly natural, conscious fear we feel when confronting physical danger. I'm talking about the unnatural, subconscious fear we feel that in one or more ways we don't have value as human beings. It's called insecurity, and it's a fear that causes nearly every self-destructive behavior. Alcoholism, drug addiction, promiscuity, overspending, undersaving: nearly every negative behavior you can think of is related to a poor self-image. It happens because beneath the surface of our minds we tend to continually hold ourselves up against a thousand yardsticks and find that we don't measure up. We're too fat. We're too old. We're not smart enough. We're not rich enough, tall enough, athletic enough. We find ourselves lacking in innumerable ways, but ultimately it all boils down to the same thing: We simply don't like ourselves enough just the way we are. So what do we do to escape these feelings? If the feelings are overwhelming, we might try to bury them with drugs, alcohol, overeating, or other self-destructive behaviors. If they're not overwhelming, we might try to make ourselves feel better by seeking validation from other people. After all, our subconscious reasons, if everybody likes me, I must be okay. If I look as rich as Donald Trump or fill out a bathing suit like Cindy Crawford, people will like and accept me, and that's hard evidence that I have value as a human being.

So what the heck does all this have to do with debt? Everything. Because lots of the ways we seek validation result in our spending money. And let me assure you, even if you've never considered your basic human insecurities, the folks on Madison Avenue think of almost nothing else. If you don't believe me, spend an hour or two watching commercials on TV. In short order, you'll learn that a certain toothpaste will make the opposite sex want to kiss you. That a certain scent will make people fall in love with you. That a certain car will make you macho. That a particular face cream will make you look younger. It's never-ending, and we're subjected to it dozens of times every day for our entire lives. Whatever the message, virtually all advertising hits us where we hurt. These ads are promising us that if we own a certain possession or use a particular product, we're going to be more valuable as human beings. And the implication would naturally follow that if we don't act as the commercials advise, we won't be as valuable. Even worse, the images these commercials present virtually guarantee that you won't measure up, because the people in them are often what our society considers extremely attractive. So even if you're totally comfortable with yourself, watch enough TV and you'll have lots of reasons not to be, unless you're a supermodel.

Result? Whether you know it or not, it's likely that at least some of these messages that pander to your insecurity are convincing you to spend money. And since it's totally absurd to think that any product can boost your self-esteem, that's money you're throwing away, because you're not getting any satisfaction in exchange. You're giving up your life, and the only ones benefiting are the companies with products to sell. The solution is to recognize these messages for the blatant manipulation they are and find your self-esteem in other places.

Only food, clothing, and shelter are more necessary to human beings than their instinctive desire to belong, to be accepted as part of a group. Because being accepted as part of a group validates us. That's one reason we're such social animals. And we not only want to be accepted as part of a group, we have a need to be recognized as an important member of that group. We've all been trained from birth that a key way people are recognized as important is by the quality and quantity of "stuff" they surround themselves with. We're taught that if you live in a nice house, wear nice clothes, and drive a nice car, then you must be successful and therefore important. But the irony is that by going into debt to appear successful, you're virtually guaranteeing that you never will be. This is the ultimate loser's game.

Envy and jealousy are also fear-based emotions that arise from insecurity. They too can cause us to spend money and go into debt. "By gosh, if John next door is driving a new BMW, I should have one, too!" "Susan makes the same money I do. If she can lie on the beach in the Bahamas, so can I." Recognize that, like the need to belong, envy, jealousy, and greed are really about fear. We're afraid that if we don't "keep up with the Joneses," we're going to be judged harshly by others and by ourselves. That's why we're so often willing to trade tomorrow's freedom so we can favorably compare ourselves to others today.

Another fear that we all share is more primitive and easier to understand. We're afraid of dying. We all recognize that, as I said in the introduction to this book, our time on this planet is limited.

And God forbid we should miss out on some experience or possession that we could have now by borrowing instead of waiting until we can actually pay for it. After all, tomorrow we could be dead. So even if that means paying three times what it costs later, best we act now before it's too late!

Do you feel angry with advertisers that pander to human insecurities, or with moneylenders? Don't. These people are only recognizing us for who we are (not a difficult task, since they're human beings, too) and transforming our natural human instincts into their corporate profits. Nothing wrong with that; that's how capitalism works. They're free to try to sell us this bill of goods. And we're just as free not to buy it. But the way to avoid it isn't to turn off your TV or focus your wrath on moneylenders. It's simply to recognize that everyone feels insecure to some degree, and the way to respond to those feelings isn't to pull out the plastic and try to spend your way to a new you. Instead, try a little acceptance.

Do you ever find yourself thinking, "What's this all about? I always thought that having a bunch of 'stuff' was what I needed to be happy. But now my home and garage are overflowing with it, and I'm not getting happier. In fact, I think I'm getting less happy!" What you're doing is waking up to the realization that you've fallen into the "buy now, feel better" trap. The whole concept of possessions making you happy is ridiculous, and you know it. Because you know that happiness comes not from physical possessions, but from loving yourself. And the only thing you need to do to love yourself is to accept yourself. Just the way you are, right now. And guess what? Acceptance is free! But we're so busy running in place pursuing "stuff" that we simply don't have the time to remember that. We're like hamsters running on a wheel, a wheel that's powered by the billions of dollars of advertising that we've been subjected to all our lives. It's time, right now, to get off the treadmill. It's time to decide to stop swapping our lives for meaningless things and instead start enriching our lives with the things we really crave. Things that are free for the taking.

Will all this work in your life? Will accepting yourself prevent you from needlessly swapping your life for meaningless possessions? Absolutely. I drive a 1982 Mercedes that I bought in 1997 for $5,800. I live in a house that's worth about half of what I could have afforded. I'm still wearing ties that I bought fifteen years ago. And despite my earlier chair example, most of the "stuff" I have was bought used, or at least as cheap as I could get it. So obviously I've found a way to satisfy my need for self-worth without having to use possessions to do it. And trust me, if I can do that, so can you. Does that mean that I don't ever fall prey to Madison Avenue? I wish! But I accept that I'll make mistakes, and I'm prepared to forgive myself when I do. I just try to stay focused on what's important: not on what my friends, co-workers, or Madison Avenue think of me, but what I think of myself. That helps me stay free of debt and in pursuit of freedom.

Bottom line? Here's something that you might already know, but if you don't, it's time you learned it. If you don't have a strong feeling of self-worth, no amount of "stuff" is going to give it to you. And if you do like yourself, just the way you are, there's no lack of "stuff" that's going to take that away. Think about that, because until you believe and embrace that concept, any attempt to change your relationship with debt and money is doomed to failure. Once you stop defining yourself by physical possessions, and recognize what you're surrendering to own them, look down. Because in your hand you're holding one of the keys you need to unlock your own financial freedom.

KEY POINTS FROM CHAPTER 3

→ When you borrow money, you're often paying three times as much for the things you buy.

→ When you spend money, you're trading your freedom and ultimately your life for the things you buy.

→ Compound interest can work just as well for you in the future as it has against you in the past.

→ If you're like most people, you stay on this spending treadmill because you simply forgot that the things that money can buy don't deliver happiness. There's another, better way to live.

CHAPTER FOUR

Financial Freedom
in Seven Days

For most of us, elementary school took six years. Junior high and high school, six more. Altogether, twelve long years of education. Then, for some of us, four or more years of college. That's a heck of a long time, yet it was time well spent, wasn't it? After all, you learned to read, to do math, to write. You learned a little about history, art, music, geography, and all the other things that help you appreciate life and civilization on planet Earth. All that education didn't make you rich or even get you a job. But it furnished your mental shed with some of the tools necessary to achieve financial security.

What school didn't teach us was some of the practical things in life. For example, how compound interest could enslave you or set you free. Or to always pay yourself before others. Or, for that matter, how to focus on your own vision of happiness instead of society's. When it comes to these kinds of things, you've been on your own all this time.

But now I'm going to ask you to step into another classroom with me, at least a mental one. Not for twelve or sixteen years, just a week. And at the end of that week, you're going to have the tools to live a life of financial freedom and abundance. You've heard the expression "Give a man a fish and you've fed him for a day; teach a man to fish and you've fed him for life." That sums up the purpose of your formal education as well as the purpose of this book. For the next seven days, you're going to learn to fish. Your debts won't be gone in a week. But for the rest of your life you're going to know how to eliminate your debts. You're going to know how saving money can not only change your life, it can change the lives of generations to come. You're going to learn how to change the failing grades on your credit history. And (added bonus!) even if you choose not to use this system, you're going to learn what's important in your life and how to appreciate it. Not bad for a few minutes a day for seven days.

If you're like me, you're going to read all seven days of lessons before you actually sit down and take the course. Good plan. But don't just read it and set it aside. Thumbing through your geometry textbook didn't teach you all the angles. At some point you had to put down the book and pick up a pencil. You had to work a problem to get it, right? Same applies here. As they say in Alcoholics Anonymous, in order for the program to work, you've got to work the program. Keep that in mind, since I'm not there to check your homework!

Debt-Free in Seven Days: Day One

Compute your average hourly after-tax, after-work-related-expenses wage. If you already did this in chapter 1, congratulations! We're just starting and you already get a day off. If you didn't, though, here's a recap of how to do it. First, multiply the amount of money you make every year by .7 to account for all the taxes you pay.

From that amount, subtract the money you spend because of your job (gas to get there, clothes you wear only there, dry-cleaning those clothes, lunches out, and so on). Take the remaining amount and divide it by 2,000. Write down that number and commit it to memory, because that's how much money you actually trade every working hour of your life for. Here's an example: I make about $100,000 per year. So $100,000 times .7 equals $70,000. Since I work primarily at home, my work-related expenses are lower than many people's, but I figure I'm still putting out $7,800 per year in lunches, suits, dry-cleaning, and travel expenses: $70,000 minus $7,800 is $62,200; $62,200 divided by 2,000 hours in a work year is $31.10, which I'll round off to $30. That's my true hourly wage.

Debt-Free in Seven Days: Day Two

Inventory your possessions. Go through your house and inventory the stuff you find there. Write down everything you see, and next to it, put its estimated cost. And don't forget the attic, the basement, the garage, any storage rooms you rent, the trunk of your car, and so forth. (This exercise is also very handy for a totally unrelated reason—you're also creating a household inventory, which is worth ten times its weight in gold should your house burn down or you're burglarized. So when you're finished with it, store it somewhere safe away from your home.)

This job will go faster for a couple if one person looks and recites while the other writes. And you don't necessarily have to list every little thing, unless you want to. In other words, you can say "dishes" or "pots and pans" or "clothes" or "living room knick-knacks" without listing each item individually. Still, even by summarizing, you may find that you can't do it all in one day. Hey, don't blame me—if you hadn't bought all that junk, it wouldn't take so long! Seriously, though, if you can't get it done in a day, take more time. In the great scheme of things, who cares whether you "graduate" in seven days or seventeen? The point is that you get where you're going, not how fast you get there.

Debt-Free in Seven Days: Day Three

Go through your household inventory, revisiting individual items if necessary, and make a mark by those that you bought but didn't really want or need. One way to identify what falls into this category is to list things you haven't touched in a year or more. But if you really want to do this right, there are lots of other things you could consider. For example, do you really need two cars? A cell phone? A health club membership? Is your house bigger than what you need? Are there tools you bought that you use so infrequently that you could have rented or borrowed them? Take extra time if you need it to really think about your life and what you've chosen to do with your money. And while you're going through your household inventory, use a highlighter to mark unwanted items so you can later either sell them or donate them to charity. The key thing here is that once you've identified the useless stuff you've accumulated, note the price you paid for each item. Add it all up. Get the total cost of all the things you thought you needed but apparently didn't.

Now multiply the total cost of your unwanted possessions by 6.7. This will tell you the opportunity cost of these things. In other words, had you invested that apparently wasted money for twenty years at 10 percent, this is how much extra you'd ultimately have had in your savings. Divide that total by the amount you actually make per hour: the after-tax, after-expenses hourly wage you figured out during day one. Now you know how many hours of financial freedom you've already lost forever by trading your time for this stuff.

Let's use an example to make sure you're picking up what I'm putting down. When we did our personal inventory here at the

Johnson house, we came up with more than $35,000 worth of un-needed or unwanted things. How did we get to this ridiculous number? It was embarrassingly easy. I had an Austin-Healey sports car that I paid $5,000 for fifteen years ago. I hadn't even seen it in seven years (it's stored at a friend's house across the country), much less driven it. We had one room of our house that we rarely even walked into. (Cost? We estimated $10,000, and that doesn't include what we pay every year to heat and cool it.) We had clothes galore. We had silver and china for all the formal entertaining that we never did. We had pieces of luggage that we never packed. We had furniture that we never sat in. ("Don't sit in that chair, it's an antique!") We were members of a dinner club that we rarely at-tended. I had a ladder and myriad tools that I bought new to save myself the hassle of borrowing from my neighbors or renting on the rare occasions when I needed them.

So what was all this extra stuff costing us in terms of our lives? Here's the math: $35,000 times 6.7 equals $234,500. That's how much we'd have had in savings if we'd invested that money at 10 per-cent for twenty years. Next, $234,500 divided by my true hourly wage of $30 equals 7,817 hours. And 7,817 divided by 40-hour weeks equals 195 weeks—that's 3 years and 9 months of work! So we dis-covered that we had already voluntarily traded nearly four years of retirement, of financial freedom, for stuff we didn't even really want. Hopefully your numbers won't be that high, but don't be surprised if they are. If you have a lower dollar amount of things you don't need, you probably also have a lower hourly wage to go with it, so your time wasted may still be numbered in years rather than weeks or months. The fact for most of us is that money wasted is in direct pro-portion to money made. In other words, no matter how much or how little money we get our hands on, we spend up to that level (if not beyond) and thereby trade a potential life of freedom for our stuff.

What's the point of this exercise? After all what you're doing here is measuring water that's already passed under the bridge. We can't get that money back, or the time it represents. But there's still a point—actually, two. One, focusing on money wasted makes us less likely to waste it in the future. The next time a shiny new widget catches your eye, you'll be less likely to buy it because you'll understand that you're swapping your life for it. Two, and more important, thinking about all the things you've accumulated is a giant step toward understanding the part that physical possessions play in your personal vision of happiness. In fact, this concept is so important that we're going to devote our entire next day to it.

Debt-Free in Seven Days: Day Four

So far, we've been doing some strenuous and somewhat depressing work: finding out how little we actually earn, adding up all the stuff we've accumulated, and discovering how much of our lives we've already surrendered to have it. Now let's change the focus to something a lot more positive and productive: finding out what really makes us happy. As you've gone through your household inventory, you've found things that you could easily have lived without. But you've also found things that you're really happy you have. The lesson for day four is to start making a list of what you really want from life.

When I went through the garage, I found my backpack. I hadn't touched it for several years, but it was hardly money wasted. Although I'm well known for my horrible memory, I can remember exactly when I bought that backpack: April 1981. I bought it because I was going on a backpacking trip across Europe. Since 1981, that backpack has been to Europe twice, South America, and Australia. It's been to the Grand Canyon twice and on innumerable other hiking and camping trips. Measured in happiness, that $75 backpack was one of the great bargains of my life, even though I haven't touched it for several years. As I dusted it off, all those memories came flooding back, and I started asking myself why I hadn't used it in so long. The answer was remarkably simple. Because I was too busy working to pay for rooms I don't use and cars I don't drive to take the time to do something I love: travel. How many camping trips had I swapped for that Austin-Healey? How many trips to exotic locales had I traded for that extra room? How many interesting people had gone unmet because of those extra clothes and that fancy china?

So here I discovered, or rather rediscovered, something that brings me joy. What joys did you rediscover as you went over your possessions? Take out a piece of paper and start painting a word picture of what makes you happy. Make a list of what these things are, then prioritize them, with the best things at the top, working your way down. If you're half of a couple, do your lists separately and don't share them until you're done. What's at the top of your list? Maybe, like mine, it's travel. But it could be something totally different. Gardening (near the top of my wife's list). Woodworking. Golf. Skydiving. Reading. Playing with children. Spending quality time with your spouse. Teaching people to read. Heck, maybe it's even working! Whatever it is, now's the time to plant it firmly in your mind by writing it down. The physical possessions you recently inventoried may, like my backpack, trigger some reminders of things you enjoy. But don't forget the other, nonmaterial things. Simply close your eyes and think about the happiest times of your life. What were you doing? Meeting new and interesting people? Telling jokes? Hugging your wife and kids? Having a picnic? Helping someone who needed it? Write down everything that comes to mind, no matter how trivial. And when you're done with your happiness list, all you have to do to have a perfect life is to stop spending money on things that don't relate directly to the activities you've written there. What you're probably going to find is that the things that make you the happiest don't involve much money. In fact, sometimes I think there's an inverse correlation between money and happiness. In other words, the more you spend, the less happiness you get.

The point of this exercise is obviously to get you refocused on what's important in your life. You may find that what brings you the greatest joy involves very little money, maybe even none at all. It may require a lot. My list, for example, includes sleeping under the stars, riding my motorcycle, sailing, meeting new and interesting people, and giving advice on TV. My wife's list includes gardening, sailing, traveling, and writing. And prominent on both our lists is laughter, especially the kind we share together. And what does all this stuff cost? Sailing isn't cheap, but we already have a sailboat (it's a $20,000 boat, but I bought it for $2,000 at an IRS auction). My Harley definitely wasn't cheap, but I get more than enough joy to justify the cost. Meeting new and interesting people goes hand in hand with travel, which doesn't have to be expensive. You don't have to fly the Concorde to get to Europe and, for that matter, you don't have to travel very far to meet fun people. Gardening isn't a huge expense. Camping is cheap. Writing is free. Being on TV actually pays money. And laughter? Free for the taking, and there will be a lot more around when I've stopped spending so much of my time and energy to buy and maintain the junk that isn't close to appearing on my happiness list.

Furniture, clothes, big houses, stereos, TVs, cars . . . these things aren't on my list. My job, and yours, is to make sure that when we're swapping our lives for money, the time we're giving up is worth it. In summary, today's exercise is the first step to aligning what's around us with what's inside us. And it's an ongoing process that lasts a lifetime. When you set your cruise control, your car isn't traveling at a steady seventy miles per hour. It's hitting sixty-nine and speeding up. It's hitting seventy-one and slowing down. Likewise, fine-tuning your happiness isn't a one-shot deal. Over time, some things will be added to your list, others will drop off. Advertising will occasionally lead you astray. So keep your list handy, and once a month or so, pull it out and check it again. That's how you'll stay focused.

Debt-Free in Seven Days: Day Five

How much money do you make every year? You used that number a few days ago when you figured out your actual hourly wage. Now use it again: multiply your annual income by .10. That amount, 10 percent of your income, is what you're going to use to pay off your debts. Divide that 10 percent by 12: this is the amount you're going to apply to your debts every month. Where's it going to come from? It's going to come from you rearranging your expenses. In other words, you're going to create a spending plan. But before you can do that, you're going to have to see where your money is going now, and that is today's task.

I've talked to many people over the years who want to set money aside, but they simply don't have any extra to do it. "How can I save when I barely have enough to make ends meet?" they say. My first response is, "Where's your money going now?" Answer: "You know . . . rent, car payment, food . . . the usual." Then I say, "Not good enough. Do you write down every single dime you spend? No? Then the fact is, you don't know where your money is going. And if you don't know where extra money is hiding, how can you find it?" As of today, you are going to write down every dime you spend. That's step one in finding the 10 percent of your income that will ultimately change your life. Once you know precisely where your money is going, you can create a spending plan so that when you do spend money, you're getting the most value possible for it.

"Hmmm . . . setting aside 10 percent of my income. Sounds like I'm about to do without something." No, you're not. You don't have to do without the experiences or things that you truly love to find your freedom money. That's why yesterday you created a list of things that make you happy.

Ever go on a diet? All the diets I see remind me of info-mercials—namely, they all promise immediate results with no effort. Some are flat-out stupid. ("Take a pill and lose unwanted pounds while you sleep!") Others seem more reasonable. Take the Atkins diet, which I've actually tried. You read the book, and good old Doc Atkins keeps repeating how you're going to be able to eat until you puke and still lose weight. And not just eat, either. You're going to be able to eat the stuff you love—lobster, butter, steaks, eggs, cream, cheese, yada yada yada. Of course, there is one tiny catch. You can't eat bread, potatoes, fruit, or anything with sugar in it. But who cares? As you're reading this book, you actually convince yourself that this is a diet you can live with. In fact, it's going to be a riot! Who needs bread when I can eat steak every night? Who needs ice cream when I can eat a burger at midnight if I want? And the book is filled with quotes from people who have lost a million pounds while eating up a storm. So you get all fired up to lose some serious weight while stuffing your face with fat. But then comes the time when the book ends and the actual diet begins. About two weeks later you're ready to murder a bird for the breadcrumb in its beak. You're so sick of burgers and eggs that passing a farm is enough to make you retch and passing a bakery makes you salivate like Pavlov's dog. Bottom line? While it may work, it ain't as easy as it sounds or, more accurately, as the author promised. And what happens is you ultimately leave it behind. (But isn't that first breadstick the best you've ever had?)

What you're about to do may seem like going on a dollar diet, but it's really not. Now, I'm not going to be an infomercial and promise you gain without pain. What I will do is promise that we can minimize the pain. How? By maintaining your lifestyle and still finding extra money to erase your debts. When you go on a diet, you might substitute cottage cheese for meat. An alternative, but one that's hard to live with, much less enjoy. But when you go on a dollar diet, you can substitute a used $100 leather chair for a new $1,000 leather chair. Your fanny is still on leather, and the substitute is virtually identical to the original, at least after a few weeks of use. So you tell me: Would you really suffer if you sat on used leather instead of new? Would it really make your life that different? I don't think so. What you've just done is free up $900 for debt reduction without negatively impacting your lifestyle one iota.

Here's another example. Stop reading this and go have a look in your medicine cabinet. If you happen to have some Excedrin (or any name-brand pain reliever) on hand, you paid more than twice what the identical generic would have cost. This is something that gives me a real headache. I've interviewed people in Walgreen's as they were actually picking up some name-brand aspirin and asked them why they were paying twice as much when inches away sat the identical product in generic form. (Notice here that I'm using the word _identical_. Generic buffered aspirin isn't close to Bayer or nearly as good as Bayer. It's identical! Read the label and you'll see for yourself.) The answers ranged from "This is what I've always bought" to "Well, if it costs more, it must be better." If there's a greater testament to advertising than those statements, I can't imagine what it is. Judging by our actions, we're apparently so concerned with Tylenol's bottom line that we're willing literally to donate several dollars to the cause every time we buy a pain reliever. Do you really think that your headache will go away faster with a name brand simply because the TV said so? If so, wake up and smell the (generic) coffee. Then start reading some labels.

One more example of how you can save money without losing your quality of life: What if you paid less for services that you can't even see? I'm talking about things like insurance or long distance. Will your neighbors be snickering behind your back because you pay seven cents a minute for long distance instead of twenty-five cents? Will your quality of life be compromised if you cut your car insurance bill by 20 percent simply by raising your deductible? Paying less for these and other services is an easy, painless way to find money for debt reduction that will give you gain without any pain. And if you think this isn't possible for many people, think again. As I write this, more than half the people using AT&T long distance are on the basic plan, which means they're paying more than twice what they'd be paying if they simply picked up the phone, called an 800 number, and asked for lower rates. Why are they paying more than necessary? Three possibilities come to mind: 1) half the people who use AT&T long distance are so rich that they have no hang-up when it comes to wasting money; 2) these people love AT&T's commercials so much that they're willing to donate money to help pay for them; or 3) they're not making the connection that pennies saved over weeks become dollars earned over months.

Bottom line? The less a diet affects your quality of life, the more likely you are to stick to it. The same thing is true for getting rid of your debt. Does that mean we can carve out 10 percent of your income for debt destruction just by smart shopping? Maybe, maybe not. Depends on how much money you're wasting now. But we can certainly produce some gain with little pain by using some commonsense techniques. And if that's not enough, we'll just have to learn to balance the pleasure we get from some of our choices against the price we're paying in money, freedom, and time. When you weigh things on that scale, could be that you end up changing the way you shop without even realizing it. In other words, you may find that some of the things that sound like deprivation today really weren't so hard to live without after all. And the pleasure you receive by becoming free and independent is so much better than the "stuff" you used to blindly trade it for.

Back to the subject at hand. Your job for today is to promise that, for at least the next month, you're going to write down every single penny you spend. Much of this work is done for you in advance, because you already record every check you write and you get statements that tell you what you bought with your credit cards. So the only thing left to account for is the cash you spend. As of today, you're going to start carrying around a little notebook and recording that cash. I'm not saying you need to spend less, at least not yet, just that you need to record what you are spending. So if you don't have a little notebook, get one. And don't leave home without it! If you don't have the opportunity to write down what you're spending as you do it, record the amounts as soon as possible thereafter. Every penny, all the time. Got it?

Debt-Free in Seven Days: Day Six

Today, you're going to continue the process of building a spending plan by seeing where your money is going now. Remember, we're going to earmark 10 percent of our income for debt reduction, which for most people will require redirecting existing expenditures to this new category. We'll be getting into more detail on this later, but for now, start collecting the paper that reveals where your money is going. In other words, pull out your checking account and credit card statements and start staring at them. What percentage of your money is going into rent or mortgage? How much are you spending on food? Utilities? Entertainment? This spending record will become more complete when you get a handle on your cash spending, which you'll do soon, since you're now recording all your cash expenditures. But today is the day to start seeing where your money is going, so you can make decisions about where your freedom money will come from.

If you want to get good at something, it helps to watch yourself do it. In the TV news business, that means watching tapes of yourself after you've done a live broadcast. But many, if not most, people in the news business don't do this, except maybe when they're just starting out. Why? Because it's uncomfortable. You see, I know that on camera I look just like Robert Redford, only smoother. And that's a self-image that's a lot easier to maintain if I'm not confronted with physical evidence to the contrary. So by not reviewing my performance, I get to leave the studio feeling smug and content, knowing that I've done good work. The only problem with this system is that if I don't look at what I've done and pick it apart, I'll never get better.

Isn't that the way most of us manage our financial lives? We know how much we make, and we know that since we're responsible, we're not spending more than we have to. God forbid we should have to confront physical evidence to the contrary. But the fact is that if we don't, we'll never get better. We'll be stuck in the same cycle that has us working for moneylenders with nothing left for ourselves. So today we're going to start reviewing our performance. We're going to see where our money is going, pick it apart, and use creative thinking to do a better job next month. We're going to make sure that we find the money for debt reduction, and we're going to make sure that the time we're swapping is worth what we're getting in return. As I said, we're going to be getting into more detail in later chapters about exactly how to do this, and there are worksheets in upcoming chapters that will help. But for now, we're going to get our feet wet by getting comfortable with the idea of reviewing what we're spending. This is a process that I guarantee will help you find the money you need to eliminate your debts forever!

Debt-Free in Seven Days: Day Seven

Now it's time to start learning the mechanics of living debt-free. That means erasing the debts you already have and avoiding them in the future. Paying off your debts will take time, but learning how doesn't take much at all. In fact, today you're going to learn the five steps required to do it. Here they are:

HOW TO TOTALLY ELIMINATE YOUR DEBTS

1. *Stop creating more debt.*
2. *Rank your debts* in order of fastest possible payoff.
3. *Build a Debt Destroyer*—set aside 10 percent or more of your gross monthly income.
4. *Pay off your debts!* Start with the debt at the top of your list. Pay the minimum monthly payment plus the Debt Destroyer amount (10 percent of your monthly gross income) to that debt until it's gone. When debt number one is gone, target debt number two on your list. For this debt, pay the minimum payment plus Debt Destroyer plus the old minimum payment from debt one. When debt number two is gone, target debt number three on your list. For this debt, pay the minimum payment plus Debt Destroyer plus the old minimum payment from debt one plus the old minimum payment from debt two. Continue with this system until all your debts are dust.
5. When all your debts are gone, *invest your Debt Destroyer plus the total of all your old monthly payments.* Convert that old Debt Destroyer into a money machine by using the money that used to create wealth for others to make you financially free!

If these steps seem a bit confusing, good. That's why this is a book and not a brochure. In the pages ahead, we're going to talk about each of these steps one at a time and see how they shake out.

We're going to use examples, and then you're going to plug in your own numbers to see how this system will work for you. But you need to become acquainted with the steps right now. So look them over and get ready to start the process. By using these simple steps, you'll become financially independent in the shortest possible time. You'll have stopped trading your life energy for someone else's profit. The money you do spend will go for the things that make you the happiest. For perhaps the first time in your life, you'll be controlling your money instead of your money controlling you. In other words, you'll be free!

If these five steps are all it takes, why not just list them and be done with it? Because just listing the steps isn't enough. What if your goal was to have a great body? I could just list the steps to get there: Work out for four hours a day and go on a diet. In fact, you already know those steps; you don't need me to tell you. But succeeding requires more than just knowing simple steps. It also takes motivation: the knowledge that you can, and will, succeed. And that's what this seven-day minicourse has been all about. It didn't even start eliminating your debts, did it? Well, maybe not, but what it did do, if you followed it, was prepare you mentally for the real deal. It laid the groundwork necessary for you to succeed as you go through the actual process. Like your formal education, it changed your way of thinking so that you had a better shot at accomplishing what you wanted.

The purpose of this seven-day preview was to get you revved up and ready to change your life from one of doubt and worry to one of happiness and abundance. Did it work?

KEY POINTS FROM CHAPTER 4

→ **Gain without pain: learning to live debt-free in seven days.**

Day one: Compute your actual hourly wage.

Day two: Inventory your possessions.

Day three: Add up the total cost of unwanted possessions. Multiply the cost by 6.7 and divide it by your actual hourly wage. This is the amount of your life you've wasted on things you didn't need.

Day four: Create a happiness list.

Day five: Start tracking your cash expenses.

Day six: Start reviewing where your money is going.

Day seven: Review the steps to getting debt-free and finding financial freedom.

→ **The steps to erasing your debts:**

1. Stop creating more debt.

2. Prioritize your debts for payoff.

3. Develop a Debt Destroyer: Set aside 10 percent or more of your gross monthly income.

4. Pay off your debts!

5. When all your debts are gone, invest your Debt Destroyer plus the total of all your old payments to build the savings that will set you free.

CHAPTER FIVE

Taking the First Step

Stop Creating More Debt!

If you want to dig a hole in your backyard, it doesn't make a lot of sense to throw in one shovelful of dirt for every two you take out. If you want to dig yourself out of debt, the first thing you've got to do is stop creating it. How? *Make it impossible to create more debt by destroying your credit cards!* Sound scary? Sure. Because those cards give you comfort. You know that if an "emergency" arises, you'll always have something to fall back on. But let me ask you something. Suppose you were going to quit smoking. Would you leave a few cartons of butts around "just in case"? If you were giving up alcohol, would you keep a bottle or two of Scotch around "just in case"? For many people, credit cards are addictive, and if you're one of these "crediholics," you've got no room in your wallet for temptation. If an emergency actually does arise, there are sources you can turn to other than credit cards. But the truth is that you're much more likely to abuse that credit card than use it to meet an emergency. And by following these steps, you'll have plenty of extra cash on hand soon enough anyway. Bottom line? *The risk of keeping those cards alive far outweighs their potential usefulness.* If an emergency actually does arise before you reach Freedom City, you can meet it by borrowing from your credit union, your employer, your parents, your 401(k) plan, or any number of other sources. If you feel cautious, make the inquiries before you slice and dice those cards so you know that the money will be there if you absolutely need it. Of course, any of these sources for emergency cash are a lot more hassle than whipping out the plastic, but that's good. Because that will encourage you to use them only in a true emergency.

Ever go to Vegas? Hang around any casino for any length of time, and you'll see tons of money changing hands. Or will you? Actually, unless you're near the cashier, you won't see *any* money changing hands. You'll see chips changing hands (more often than not, from your hands to the dealer's). Why do casinos use chips instead of real money? Because they know that you're much more likely to wager pieces of plastic than "real" money. And, of course, they also know that the odds are in their favor—that if you hang around long enough, more of those pieces of plastic will end up on their side of the table than yours. And just to make sure you stay long enough, they'll even happily ply you with free alcohol and eliminate unnecessary distractions like clocks and windows. In many ways, credit cards are like that. *It's a fact that you're going to spend more money by exchanging plastic for stuff than you would if you were paying with cash.* And the more you spend, the more likely it is that you'll go into debt. And the more you go into debt, the more moneylenders make. Too bad they can't get you drunk before you go to the mall!

If you ever visit Las Vegas, you'll be amazed by the size and opulence of the megacasinos on the strip. Some of the money used to build and maintain these casinos comes from selling food, liquor, and souvenirs or renting rooms. But the vast majority of it comes from people voluntarily donating their money by playing games in which they should know the odds are against them. And if you ever take a trip to New York City, visit the headquarters of the major banks. You'll be amazed by the size and opulence of these buildings. Some of the money used to build and maintain them comes from the fees they charge for checking accounts and such. But the vast majority of it comes from people donating their money by playing a credit game in which they should know the odds are against them. *Both of these games, gambling and moneylending, are hugely profitable for the house because they find so many losers to play them. Don't be a loser. Cut up your credit cards!*

"But wait!" you say. "Credit cards offer more than just a way for lenders to get me to buy stuff I don't need and borrow the money to do it. They also offer convenience. After all, if there's something I need on the Internet or Home Shopping, I can't exactly cram dollar bills into the computer or the phone. Besides, carrying cash isn't safe." Okay, good points. There are two substitutes that will work just fine when plastic is a necessity. The best one is a debit card. It looks, acts, feels, tastes, and smells just like a credit card, but there's an important difference. A debit card takes the money directly out of your checking account, so it's basically like using cash. Another possibility is to use a traditional American Express card, because it doesn't allow you to carry a balance. So there are ways to access the convenience of plastic without the debt risk. And as to the safety of carrying cash? No doubt you're better off not walking around downtown with a wad of bills in your pocket. But who says you need to walk around with a lot of cash all the time? If you're going to the store to buy a pair of pants, take enough money to pay for the pants. If you're going to the grocery store, take enough to buy what you need. That's the absolute best way to prevent impulse buying. Take a look around your house and focus especially on your closets. Notice all that stuff you have that you never use? All those clothes hanging in those closets that you never wear? Odds are most of it is a direct result of impulse buying. *Had you gone to the store the days you bought that stuff carrying only the cash required to buy what you went there for, you'd have avoided much of the debt you now have.* That's why I'd rather see you using cash than a check, debit card, or no-balance credit card. It simply makes it difficult to buy things you don't really need or want.

KEY POINTS FROM CHAPTER 5

→ You can't get rid of old debt until you're committed to stop creating new debt.

→ Arrange for other sources of emergency cash first.

→ Keep the convenience of plastic without the risk of credit cards by using a debit card or no-balance-allowed charge card.

→ Carry cash: you'll spend less money by avoiding impulse buys.

CHAPTER SIX

Rank Your Debts for Payoff

This chapter is all about getting organized and deciding which debts we're going to pay off first. If you're already on a debt management plan (DMP) with a credit counseling organization (explained in chapter 12), you can skip this chapter and head for chapter seven. But if you're going it alone, let's get going!

Since the goal is to pay off debts, let's start by defining exactly what a "debt" is. It's something you owe that you can theoretically stop owing. For example, your mortgage is a debt. But your property taxes aren't a debt; they're an ongoing expense. Your Visa bill is a debt. Your utility bills aren't. Your car loan is a debt, but your car insurance bill is an expense. Okay? Now, the first thing you need to do is make a list of your debts. So stop reading, dig those bills out of the drawer, grab your check register, and let's get started.

A special note for readers who hate numbers and are scared of tables and such: I know just looking at charts and graphs can immediately convert many otherwise normal folks into zombies.

But I can't really explain this stuff just by talking about it. I've got to give you some example numbers, and you've got to write down your own. So if you're the type who always gets that thousand-yard stare when numbers enter the act, it's time to get over it. Trust me, there are people a lot dumber than you who do this, and after a while it can even get to be fun! (Well, maybe "fun" is an exaggeration, but you can't blame a guy for trying.)

Throughout this process I'm going to be giving you a sample table first, then a blank one so you can do the calculations yourself with your own real-life info. The sample information comes to us courtesy of my favorite fictitious family, Sam and Sally Sample. (What a coincidence!) Since we're going to be referring to them often, let's get to know them a little bit. Sam and Sally Sample both come from middle-class families in the Midwest. They met in college and dated heavily pretty much the whole time, but they waited until after graduation to tie the knot. While they didn't grow up anywhere near each other, they might as well have, since they both come from very similar backgrounds. Despite a little help from their parents, both Sam and Sally had to pay most of their own college expenses. As a result, they endured some hardship during school, at least financially. For Sam, paying the rent was always a problem, much less paying tuition and finding the money to impress Sally. For her part, Sally stayed in the dorm until her senior year, when she moved into an apartment with three girlfriends. Despite the hardships, Sally made it through school in four years. Sam took six, because there were several times he had to quit and work for a while. But he didn't mind that, since he knew he had the discipline to finish, and he didn't want to have too much debt when he got out.

Sam and Sally got married less than a week after graduation. It was the happiest day of their lives. Both Sam and Sally couldn't wait to start their life together. They knew that they wanted a family, and after years of deprivation, they were definitely ready to start living the American dream. Sam got a job right out of college with the Shapely Shake Shingle Company. He started with an annual salary of $24,000, but now, six years later, he's making close to $30,000. Sally was working full-time selling seashells by the seashore until little Samantha came along a few years ago. Now Sally works part-time but still makes about $20,000 a year.

Like many young couples, Sam and Sally started out with basically nothing. In fact, they started out with actually less than nothing, since Sally came into the marriage with a student loan. At least Sally's parents gave her an old car as a graduation present; Sam shared that car at first but finally got his own a couple of years ago. Both Sam and Sally consider themselves good money managers, and they pretty much stay on top of what's happening moneywise. Sally writes most of the household checks, but not because Sam doesn't know how or isn't interested. It's just easier for Sally, since she's at home a lot of the time with three-year-old Samantha. They've had spats about money before, but disagreements are basically rare. While they each have their own credit cards, they try to keep the balances down and discuss it if they feel the need for a major purchase.

But now, six years into their marriage, Sam and Sally Sample are starting to feel a little less than satisfied. They don't exactly have money problems, but at the same time, on those few occasions when they stop to think about it, they're concerned. Their credit card balances seem to be creeping skyward despite the fact that they're now bringing in about $50,000 a year between the two of them. And the thing that's the most disheartening is that their financial freedom is nowhere in sight. It's also odd and a bit ironic that while they certainly have more "stuff" than they had when they met, including their own home, they seem to be enjoying life less than when they were poor college students. Sam is getting tired of selling shake shingles, but he doesn't know where else he can go to immediately to make as much money. Sally likes selling seashells, but she's wondering why she's working for someone else who doesn't know nearly as much as she does about them. She often fantasizes about owning her own seashell shop at the seashore. Of course, little Samantha is a joy, but Sam and Sally agree that when college time rolls around for her, they don't want her to struggle as they did. And they have yet to start saving any money for Samantha's education.

Sam and Sally don't have any debt or a money crisis in the traditional sense. But they're wondering where their "get up and go" got up and went. When they look down the road, they see more of the same: collecting possessions that bring them less and less joy and gradually surrendering the dreams they shared when they started out. They're feeling trapped working in jobs that don't make them happy, with no way to change the situation. When they were in school, they had their whole lives ahead of them, with nowhere to go financially but up. They still have practically their whole lives ahead of them, but their dreams of financial freedom are fading. That's why they've come to us for help, and we're going to turn them around.

The first thing we did with Sam and Sally is get them to agree to stop using debt. In other words, step one. Now it's time for step two: We're going to help Sam and Sally figure out where they are today. Sam and Sally bought their house four years ago with an 8 percent, thirty-year mortgage that started out at $125,000. Now the balance is down to about $120,000. Sam's car came equipped with a loan that's about a year and a half old. It's a 10 percent, five-year loan that started off at $10,000 and is now around $7,500. Sally has a student loan that charges 8 percent, started at $15,000, and runs for ten years. She started paying on it about three years ago, and the balance is now about $11,700. Both of their credit cards charge 15 percent and require minimum monthly payments of the greater of 2 percent or $10.

To get a clearer picture of Sam and Sally's finances, let's have them put down exactly whom they owe money to, how much they owe, and how much the minimum payments are. Here's what it looked like after they sat down and listed their debts. Think of it as a family picture of where they are debtwise right this minute.

DEBT TABLE: THE SAMPLE FAMILY				
DEBT	CURRENT BALANCE	MINIMUM PAYMENT	COLUMN 2 DIVIDED BY COLUMN 3	DEBT RANK
Sam's Visa card	$2,239	$45		
Sally's MasterCard	$1,845	$37		
Sam's car loan	$7,500	$212		
Sally's student loan	$11,700	$182		
Mortgage loan	$120,000	$917		

Now, how about going through this exercise yourself? As you're listing your debts, remember that sometimes you might have other stuff included in bill payments that you don't want to consider. For example, Sam and Sally actually pay more than $917 on their mortgage, because every payment includes some extra money for real estate taxes and homeowners insurance. The $917 is just for principal and interest on their loan. And since, as we noted earlier, insurance and taxes are expenses, not debts, they have to be taken out. Sam found the current mortgage balance and the principal and interest part of the payment by looking at their annual mortgage statement. Getting the necessary amounts for the credit cards was simple enough: Sally just pulled out the latest bills. To find out the current balance on the student and car loans, they had to call the companies because their dog, Spot, had eaten their annual statements (at least that's what they told me). They also rounded off the numbers. That's fine: you don't have to be precise to the penny.

Now it's your turn. Write down your debts. Include the company or person you owe the money to, how much it is, and what the minimum monthly payments are—in other words, columns 1, 2, and 3. Ignore the other two columns just now; we'll get to them in a minute.

MY DEBTS AS OF _____				
DEBT	CURRENT BALANCE	MINIMUM PAYMENT	COLUMN 2 DIVIDED BY COLUMN 3	DEBT RANK

Rank Your Debts for Payoff

Got it done? Way to go! Now we'll do something easy . . . whip out the old calculator and divide the amount you owe by the minimum monthly payment (in other words, column 2 divided by column 3) and put the answer in column 4. Here's what it looked like when Sam and Sally did it:

PAYMENTS LEFT: THE SAMPLE FAMILY				
DEBT	CURRENT BALANCE	MINIMUM PAYMENT	COLUMN 2 DIVIDED BY COLUMN 3	DEBT RANK
Sam's Visa card	$2,239	$45	50	
Sally's MasterCard	$1,845	$37	50	
Sam's car loan	$7,500	$212	35	
Sally's student loan	$11,700	$182	64	
Mortgage loan	$120,000	$917	131	

Now it's your turn! Go back to your table, divide your current balances by your minimum payments, and write the answer in the fourth column.

Got it done? Okay, now all that's left is ranking your debts in the order that they're going to be paid off. The lowest number is going to the highest place on the list: it's going to be number one. So let's see how Sam and Sally's list looks:

DEBT RANKING: THE SAMPLE FAMILY				
DEBT	CURRENT BALANCE	MINIMUM PAYMENT	COLUMN 2 DIVIDED BY COLUMN 3	DEBT RANK
Sam's Visa card	$2,239	$45	50	2
Sally's MasterCard	$1,845	$37	50	2
Sam's car loan	$7,500	$212	35	1
Sally's student loan	$11,700	$182	64	3
Mortgage loan	$120,000	$917	131	4

So, for Sam and Sally, their priority one debt will become the car loan. Then we've got a tie for number two on the credit cards, followed by Sally's student loan, and, bringing up the rear, the mortgage loan.

What does your priority list look like? Go back and finish the debt table by ranking your debts.

Now we've made a list of all of our debts, and we know which debt we're going to target first, second, and so on. Two steps down, three to go: we're already almost halfway to Freedom City! But before you go on to the next chapter to continue down the list of steps, you might have a couple of questions about why we ranked our debts this way and if other ways of ranking them would have worked. So before you ask those questions, I'll answer 'em.

The first thing you should understand is that the system we're using is designed to keep you on track by giving you the most reward in the fastest time. In other words, while we can't compete with Madison Avenue by promising you instant gratification, we're going to do the best we can to get you results as soon as possible, which we hope will get you excited and keep you going. When you divide the amount of your monthly payments into the amount of each debt, what you're going to get is the number of payments you have left until that debt is gone. Focusing on the debt with the fewest monthly payments left means it will be gone the quickest, and you'll see fast results from your efforts. That's important both for inspiration and because you'll free up more money as quickly as possible—money that we need to wipe out the next debt on your list in record time.

Now maybe you're saying, "Hold on there, partner! If we're interested in making rapid progress, why not focus on the littlest debt first?" Well, because when debt one is gone, we're going to be using those old payment amounts on debt two anyway. Besides, keep in mind that the way principal and interest is figured on long-term loans, most of the money in the early years is interest, and most of the money in the later years is principal. So if you've got an old loan with high payments, odds are that more of each payment is going to principal, which means that adding to that payment will erase that debt even faster. And erasing those debts fast is what we're all about!

Another question you might have: Why not focus on the debts in order of interest rate? Doesn't it make sense to pay off a 15 percent debt before a 10 percent debt? Actually, yes. But again, we're trying to get you out of debt as soon as possible, and we're going to be using the old payments from erased debts to do it. This system will work so fast for you that the small amount of extra interest you'll end up paying won't amount to much anyway. It's worth it to show you quick progress.

One more question: What if I wanted to ignore the way you're ranking my debts and use a different system, like first paying the smallest debt or the ones with the highest interest rate? Would the system still work? Sure. Maybe not exactly as fast, but it will still work. So if you want to get picky, go ahead and see if I care! The main thing is that you follow the other steps and get the heck out of debt so you can start living life as a free person.

KEY POINTS FROM CHAPTER 6

→ Dig out your statements and list all your debts.

→ Divide the balance you still owe by the minimum monthly payment. That gives you the number of months left to pay off a debt.

→ Rank your debts. The debt with the least number of payments left is the first one that gets paid off.

→ The reason we're attacking our debts this way is that it rewards us faster, which provides both motivation and more money to add to our Debt Destroyer.

CHAPTER SEVEN

Creating Your Debt Destroyer

Okay, now we've spent some time looking at our situation. In step one, we agreed to stop taking on new debt, and in step two we've made a list of what we owe, whom we owe it to, and how much our payments are. We also decided what order we're going to use to pay off our debts. Now it's time for step three: Let's create a weapon to destroy our debts!

If you're going to attack a powerful enemy, you use every weapon at your disposal. Ever watch cops at work? Arresting violent, dangerous people is risky business, so to minimize their personal risk, they use a powerful combination of mental and physical weapons. Mentally, they're alert, prepared, and well trained. They know exactly what steps to take to conclude confrontations quickly, safely, and successfully. Physically, they do what is necessary to make sure they have the upper hand. Want to use your fists? They'll use a nightstick or Mace. Want to use a knife? They'll use a gun. Want to use a gun? They'll show up with three hundred. In other words, these are people who clearly understand that the way to win is to keep a sharp mental edge and an overwhelming physical one.

What we're essentially doing with step three is taking a lesson from the cops and developing our own mental and physical arsenal to subdue and ultimately exterminate debt. In the introduction and chapter 1, we started sharpening our mental edge when we took the time to understand how we came by the debts we have. We recognized how moneylenders pander to our human nature and encourage us to trade our most precious possession, our lives, for their profit. We accepted that our freedom of choice is at stake, and we chose to do whatever it takes to create and maintain that freedom for ourselves. In chapters 2, 3, and 4, we started training to deal with debt. We learned how to stop adding to the problem by creating more debt, and we made a list of our debts, then ranked them in the order we're going to pay them off. Now it's time to pull out the big gun and start putting that debt out of your misery. We call that big gun a Debt Destroyer.

Your Debt Destroyer is simply a wad of cash equal to 10 percent of your gross monthly income. You're going to aim this powerful weapon at the first debt on your list, add it to the existing minimum payment, and pull the trigger every month until that debt disappears. Obviously, you've got to be wondering, "How the heck am I supposed to scrounge up 10 percent of my income every month?" Well, the answer to that question is all around you. Let's look for it until we find it.

In order to set aside 10 percent of your monthly income, the first thing you've got to do is figure out how much that number is. So if you didn't do it before, do it now. Start with how much you make a year. (This you'll probably know right off the top of your head. Although most of us develop amnesia when it comes to knowing what we owe, we're sharp as tacks when it comes to knowing what we make.) Divide that number by 12, then multiply that number by .1, and you're there. For example, Sam and Sally Sample have a combined income of $50,000 a year. So their monthly income is $4,167 ($50,000 divided by 12), and their Debt Destroyer amount is going to be $417 ($4,167 times .1).

Where will Sam and Sally find $417 every month? Well, they can't find it if they don't know where to look, and they won't know where to look until they know where their money's going. Which means, yes, it's now time for the dreaded "b" word! Sam and Sally have to have a budget. Actually, let's avoid the word *budget*, because budget implies deprivation, like the word *diet*. What Sam and Sally are actually going to do is develop a spending plan. In other words, they're going to make conscious and completely voluntary decisions about how to allocate their money. Diets and budgets deprive us of things we want so that we can lose weight or save money. A spending plan isn't about deprivation. It's about aligning where your money is going with your personal vision of happiness.

So Sam and Sally's spending plan doesn't mean doing without, it simply means paying attention and setting a few priorities. You start by *keeping track of where your money's going*, which we already started doing in Chapter 4. Once you've done that, you're in a position to make decisions about how to allocate your money and spend it according to your personal priorities. And one of your priorities is going to be funneling money to build your Debt Destroyer. In fact, that's going to be your top priority!

So here's the drill: Until you feel comfortable coming up with your Debt Destroyer each and every month, write down everything you spend. Every penny, every day. A lot of this you're already doing. When you write a check, you're obviously writing down the amount and payee in your check register, right? When you use a debit or credit card, it shows up on your statement. When you have money taken out of your paycheck, it shows up on your check stub. So when we talk about keeping track of every dime you spend, what we're really talking about is where your cash is going. The way to keep track of it is to carry around a small notebook and simply make a note of the amount and what you buy whenever you spend cash. You'll get used to it in no time, and it's actually not that much of a hassle. Then once a month, put all the numbers together on paper and categorize them.

Here's an example of what it looked like when Sam and Sally wrote down or otherwise gathered all their expenses in their quest for a Debt Destroyer. Notice they also included some notes so they'd remember where they put certain amounts.

WHERE SAM AND SALLY'S MONEY IS GOING

MONTHLY EXPENSE	AMOUNT	NOTES
Bill payments	$1,393	This includes principal and interest on the mortgage, along with all other minimum loan payments.
Savings	$250	$200/month for Sam's 401(k) plan, $50/month for Sally's savings.
Eating out	$190	Includes work lunches out and eating out.
Entertainment	$220	Includes the cable TV bill, video rentals, alcohol (both in and out), bowling league, golf, health club, on-line computer services, CDs, books, and magazines
Groceries	$300	Includes cleaning and laundry stuff and Spot's food
Clothes	$100	

Creating Your Debt Destroyer

MONTHLY EXPENSE	AMOUNT	NOTES
Utilities	$140	Includes phone, water, gas, and electricity
Real estate taxes	$60	$1/12$ of the amount from the annual mortgage statement
Home insurance	$30	$1/12$ of the amount from the annual mortgage statement
Health insurance	$100	From Sam's check stub
Life insurance	$50	Sam's policy
Child care	$140	Sally's sitter
Transportation	$100	Includes gas, maintenance, parking, and tolls
Home maintenance	$40	Includes lawn care and tools
Charity	$50	Church, United Way, and stuff we buy from neighbor kids
Other stuff	$100	Includes gifts, furniture, and misc. irregular expenses
Total	**$3,263**	

There are lots of things we can learn by looking at this list of Sam and Sally's cash outlays for the month. The first thing we might notice, for example, is that they spent pretty much everything they made, at least this month. Remember, their combined pay before taxes is $4,167. But after taxes, they're bringing home only about $3,500, so that's obviously all they have to spend. Of course, they also saved $250 and gave $50 to charity, so when you consider that, they're really doing okay. But as you'll soon see, they also have some expenses coming up that aren't on this list that will make later months more expensive. So while this month looks pretty good, it also could actually help explain why they have more than $4,000 on their credit cards. Because in those months when they have more month than money, that's what they use to support their life-style. And what happens if there's a minor disaster? Say Sally's car needs a $600 valve job, for instance. Where's that money coming from? Not from Sam's retirement account. So maybe Sally raids her meager savings, but because she's hesitant to touch her "emergency money," it's more likely that she uses the Visa. The Visa will also come into play when it's time for new furniture, a vacation, or that occasional trip to the mall.

Anyway, now that we know what they spent, we'll add a couple of lines and columns to the expense list and create a spending plan. There aren't many differences between the two when you look at them. But there's a mongo difference conceptually. Because a spending plan introduces you to prioritizing. In other words, it lets you set an ideal amount for each category of your expenses. Then, when the month is over, you compare what you actually spent to what you thought you would or wanted to spend and fine-tune it accordingly. "Could I have spent less on food? Probably . . . let's try to reduce that amount next month by $10 and see what hap-pens." "Think I'll reduce the transportation expense by $20 this month and see if I can hit that. Hmmm . . . what if I carpooled once a week?" So creating a spending plan is important because that's when you stop just looking at what you're doing and start changing it. It's also when you begin to learn what it is that makes you happy and what doesn't; what's *really* important to you and what was something you just *thought* was important. For example, Sam's been bowling for seven years with the same group of guys. He loves these guys, and he loves bowling. Sure, if he gave up bowling, he'd save $15 a week, which, should he invest it, could become $50,000 twenty years from now. But even at that price, it's not worth it to give up bowling! Cool. That's fine. We've discovered something that Sam's willing to trade for the money and the time it costs him. On the other hand, maybe he looks at the golf expense and says, "I thought golf would be fun, but the truth is it's too time-consuming and I don't really even like it that much anyway. I think I would rather have the $50,000 twenty years from now. I'm cutting it out of the plan." Has Sam ruined his quality of life? Not in any way. In fact, he's added to his quality of life in at least three ways: one, he's now going to be richer; two, he's thought about and appreciated the things that bring him true joy; three, he's stopped doing things that he doesn't like doing, which gives him more time to do the things he does.

Let's stop here and take a look at how Sam and Sally convert their list of money spent monthly into a spending plan. Then we can talk about a couple of other things.

SAM AND SALLY'S STARTING SPENDING PLAN				
MONTHLY EXPENSE	ACTUAL	PLAN	DIFFERENCE	NOTES
Bill payments	$1,393	$1,393		
Savings	$250	$250		
Eating out	$190	$190		
Entertainment	$220	$220		
Groceries	$300	$300		
Clothes	$100	$100		
Utilities	$140	$140		

MONTHLY EXPENSE	ACTUAL	PLAN	DIFFERENCE	NOTES
Real estate taxes	$60	$60		
Home insurance	$30	$30		
Health insurance	$100	$100		
Life insurance	$50	$50		
Child care	$140	$140		
Transportation	$100	$100		
Home maintenance	$40	$40		
Charity	$50	$50		
Other stuff	$100	$100		
Car insurance	0	$92		
Emergency spending	0	$100		
Debt Destroyer	0	$417		
Total	**$3,263**	**$3,872**		

As you can see, Sam and Sally's starting plan is simply their expenses with a couple of extra lines and columns thrown in. One thing that's important to add to your spending plan is expenses that you know are going to happen but aren't going to happen every month. Example? Third from the bottom we've added an expense for car insurance. Sam and Sally obviously have a car insurance bill, but it happens every six months, not every month.

Still, they don't want to forget about it, so they put it in their plan. This is one area that many people mess up when they look over their expenses. They take a look at the last few weeks and forget the expenses they haven't had to write a check for during that time. That makes the short-term look sweet, but when that semi-annual bill comes in, they suddenly find that their money picture isn't quite as rosy as they thought. Don't make that mistake. Think about all your expenses, and don't forget to look ahead and behind on the calendar to find and account for them.

The next-to-last expense category is emergency spending. That's for expenses we know we're going to have, we just don't know what to call them yet. Sam's going to sit on his glasses. Sally's going to suddenly remember the extravagant gift she has to buy for her niece's wedding. Samantha's going to need to go to the orthodontist. Spot's going to need to go to the vet. Bottom line? Just because we can't guess what all our surprise expenses might be doesn't mean we shouldn't acknowledge their existence. So when you start putting together your own spending plan, don't forget that. It's life's little surprises that often separate a plan that looks good but doesn't work from one that you can use. And of course, we've also added one last expense line, Debt Destroyer. When we add all these expenses together, you can see that Sam and Sally are now planning to spend $3,872, which is obviously not doable. So they've got to go back and adjust their expense plan to make room for the new expenses they've added, especially the Debt Destroyer!

Before we go on, let's give you a place to write down your expenses for the next month and a place to start your own spending plan. Make copies of these sheets so you can have blank ones to use in future months as well. Since everybody's different, you might need more or different categories from the ones we've listed here. If so, make your own. It doesn't have to look neat, it just has to accurately account for where your money's going.

MONTHLY EXPENDITURES AND SPENDING PLAN
FOR THE MONTH OF _____

MONTHLY EXPENSE	ACTUAL	PLAN	DIFFERENCE	NOTES
Bill payments				
Savings				
Eating out				
Entertainment				
Groceries				
Clothes				
Utilities				
Real estate taxes				
Home insurance				
Health insurance				
Life insurance				
Child care				
Transportation				
Home maintenance				
Charity				
Other stuff				
Car insurance				

MONTHLY EXPENSE	ACTUAL	PLAN	DIFFERENCE	NOTES
Emergency spending				
Debt Destroyer				
Total				

Now, let's get back to the subject at hand—namely, how to create a 10-percent-of-income Debt Destroyer when we barely have enough to make it as it is. Before we do that, however, let's pause for a quick goal refresher by pondering Sam and Sally's first expenditure item: the $1,393 they pay on loans every month. If they didn't have to make those payments, they'd have plenty of money left over, wouldn't they? And what if they invested that money every month and made, say, 10 percent on it? Well, after twenty years (they'd be in their late forties at that time) they'd have $1,068,008! So imagine how different their situation would look—$1,393 less in bills every month and a million bucks in savings. Think that would qualify as financially free?

Okay, back to reality. Remember, we're looking for 10 percent of gross income or, in Sam and Sally's case, $417. Turn back to their spending plan and let's look at it together and see if we can find that magic money. Hmmm . . . what about the money they're putting in savings? That's a good place to start. Because there's no way that the money that's going into savings is earning more than the interest they're paying on debts. Plus, they have to pay taxes on the savings interest they're earning, and they don't get to deduct the debt interest they're paying, except for the mortgage. So here's a good place to start our Debt Destroyer: with money that's now going into savings. In Sam and Sally's case, that's $250.

"But wait!" you say. "Everything I've ever read about smart financial planning says you should always save something out of every paycheck. What about the old 'pay yourself first' idea?" Well, it is a good idea to save, and remember, saving money every month will once again become a priority, *after our debts are gone.* But why would we pay 15 percent interest on a credit card when we're earning only 5 percent in a savings account (which is actually only about 3–4 percent after taxes)? We shouldn't, and for this program we won't. *This program is temporary.* It's designed to get us out of debt as soon as possible. We're going to use every available weapon in our arsenal to succeed. Before Sam and Sally started this program, Sam went to his credit union, talked to a loan officer, and made sure that he could borrow money if it was an absolute emergency. He also talked to the human resources person at his job to inquire about loans from his 401(k). Sally even told her parents what she and Sam were up to and asked if they'd be willing to help should she and Sam find themselves in dire straits. So before these guys even took the first step (cutting up those credit cards), they made sure they had their emergency bases covered.

But, as with most rules, there is an exception to this one. Because there is one situation where we don't divert our savings dollars to build a Debt Destroyer, and it's one that affects Sam and Sally. Namely, when we're getting matching dollars from our employer in a 401(k) or other voluntary retirement plan, *we make sure we get the full match before we reduce those contributions.* Why? Well, consider Sam's situation. For every dollar that he puts into his 401(k) plan, his company puts in fifty cents, up to 6 percent of Sam's salary. And by getting that match, he's earning an immediate 50 percent on his savings! That's pretty tough to beat, especially when you consider that it's risk-free. So let's take another look at Sam's situation. He makes $30,000 per year; 6 percent of $30,000 is $1,800. That's the most Sam's employer will give matching dollars for, no matter how much Sam contributes to the plan. Bottom line? Sam needs to continue contributing $1,800 per year, or $150 per month, to make sure he gets that easy, safe 50 percent return. Since he's now contributing $200 a month, he can reduce that amount by $50 and use it for their Debt Destroyer. And Sally can contribute her $50 savings. We're going to reduce the savings amount from $250 a month to $150 a month and put the difference in the Debt Destroyer row.

So now we've found $100 for our Debt Destroyer. How about the other $317? Well, we can temporarily stop donating to charity. Sam and Sally shouldn't feel an ounce of guilt about this. They know the plan isn't permanent, and when it's over, they'll be in a position to help their favorite causes much more effectively, in terms of donating both money and their time. We agree to reduce the charity amount to zero and add that money to the Debt Destroyer.

Okay, another $50 down, but we still need to find an additional $267. Let's take a look again at their list of expenditures and see what else we can do. There are probably at least one hundred different ways that we can find more money, and there's a ton of them coming in a later chapter, but let's explore a few simple ideas right now. Remember, earlier in the book I talked about saving money painlessly. What we want to do is reduce Sam and Sally's expenses without reducing their quality of life. So here's a question I'll propose to Sam: Would you really suffer if you ate a lunch from home every day instead of always eating out? If you spend $5 a day eating out, that's $25 a week or about $100 a month. Bringing lunch from home would cost no more than half that amount. Savings: $50 a month. So we can reduce the eating-out amount by $50 and add that amount to their Debt Destroyer.

Now we're down to $217 still left to find. Here's another simple thing that these two could consider: the health club. They're paying $37 a month to that health club, and even if they're health freaks, that's unnecessary money. Why? Well, I try to stay in shape, too, and I don't belong to a health club. I went down to Blockbuster and bought two workout tapes (*Arms of Steel* and *Abs of Steel*, if you must know) for $7 apiece. I work out in front of my TV for nothing. And what's more healthy (and less expensive) than jogging in the fresh air? Sam and Sally agree. Another $37 freed up. We reduce the entertainment amount by $37 and add that much to the Debt Destroyer. And now we're looking for only $180 more.

The entertainment category is a place where we can continue to look for savings. At this point, perhaps it's time to mention one of the greatest places in the world when it comes to saving money: the public library. Here's a question for Sam, Sally, and you: How many times do you reread books? I rarely do (with the notable exception of this one!). Yet most of us will drive farther to a bookstore to pay a high price for a book that we're going to use only once than we would driving to the library to get the same book for free! Result? When we're done reading that purchased book, it's magically transformed from entertainment into dust-collecting clutter, and the money we paid for it is transformed from our freedom to a publisher's profit. And did you know the library also has video and music tapes and CDs, also for free? Think of it . . . through our taxes, we're already paying for a big chunk of the world's information and entertainment, yet rarely does it cross our minds to visit our own local library. Know why? Because the library doesn't have a big advertising budget!

Sam and Sally agree that they might be able to circumvent a few trips to the bookstore and Blockbuster by going to the library. Savings: $25 per month. Out it comes from the entertainment expense, and in it goes to the Debt Destroyer. Now just $155 to go.

What about the cable bill? "Hold on there!" says Sam. "I *need* cable!" No sweat. But what about all the premium channels? Do you really need three HBOs and two Cinemaxes? Not likely. Usually those channels are filled with two kinds of movies anyway: those you've already seen and those you never wanted to see in the first place. Besides, reading is much more fun and certainly sets a better example for little Samantha. Sam agrees that he hardly ever watches the premium channels. And if they really want to see a recent movie, they can either find it at the library, rent it from a video store, or do the pay-per-view thing. "True," he agrees. Okay, let's cut out the premium channels and see if they can do without them. If not, there's no law against resubscribing. That carves another $20 out of the entertainment expense, adds it to the Debt Destroyer, and means we're now looking for $135.

Okay, let's take a look at groceries. Sally's eyebrows shoot skyward as this topic comes up. "I do the best I can with the grocery bill!" she exclaims. I'm sure she does, and you do, too. In fact, I doubt anyone goes to the grocery store trying to spend as much as possible and get as little as possible in return. But the fact remains that there are so many ways to save on food that complete books have been written on that topic alone. For example, does Sally *always* buy generic items whenever they'll do the exact same job? Some people shun generics because they assume the quality is worse. And guess what? They are worse in many cases. And those are the cases where you avoid generics. But do you think bleach is worse if it isn't Clorox? Do you think your quality of life will be hurt if salt isn't Morton's? Do you think aspirin won't work if it isn't Bayer? Generics in such staples as patent medicine, toiletries, cleaning products, and many kinds of food can save you up to 50 percent, and you won't be able to tell the difference at all. And that's the tip of the iceberg when it comes to saving money on consumables. For example, Sally also admitted that she didn't often use a list when she shopped. Using a list can save you 10 percent. You've got plenty more ideas ahead in a later chapter. The point is, Sally agreed to at least try to reduce the grocery bill by 10 percent. The food amount goes down by $34, the Debt Destroyer goes up by $34. Now we need only $101.

Ever notice how much you spend on insurance? You will when you start finding out where all your money goes. Sam and Sally spend $272 every month insuring their home, their cars, their health, and Sam's life. That's about 8 percent of all the money that ever makes its way into their lives—almost as much as they spend on food!

Insurance is nearly the ideal business, as long as you're an insurance company and not a consumer. Why? Well, think about it. Here's a business that's taking nearly one dollar of every ten that Sam and Sally ever see, yet they rarely even think about it, much less shop it around or otherwise try to minimize the expense. And why don't they do that? Because it's complicated, it's required (in the case of their home and cars, at least), and it's invisible. They hardly ever think about their insurance coverages, and when they do, they feel kind of helpless because they don't even know what questions to ask in order to get it for less.

Well, let's consider a few basic facts about insurance to help Sam and Sally stop voluntarily donating so much of their lives to pay for it. The purpose of insurance is to prevent a nasty surprise from ruining your life financially. Notice I said "ruining," not "inconveniencing." Despite what the insurance industry would have you believe, the purpose of insurance is not to remove all the risk from your life. If you want to insure yourself so that you'll never lose a dollar, you'll be paying so much for insurance that you may never end up with a dollar to lose!

Sam and Sally have very low deductibles ($250) on their homeowners and car insurance policies. That means they're responsible for the first $250 of loss, then the insurance company covers the rest. Sounds good, but they're also paying 20 percent more for these policies than an identical policy with a $1,000 deductible. So if they're willing to take a little more risk, they'll pay a lot less money. If disaster strikes, would losing $1,000 instead of just $250 ruin their lives financially? Of course not. A bummer, certainly, but it wouldn't put them in the poorhouse. They are also paying for insurance "frills" that they never use, like roadside towing on their car policy. Sounds good, but have they ever, even once, used it? Nope. The dental insurance that comes as a part of Sam's medical insurance is another example of where the cost of the coverage exceeds any real value they could get from it. Why? Because other than an annual cleaning, it doesn't really cover all that much anyway. And it costs an extra $25 per month.

Almost everyone pays too much for insurance because they don't shop it often enough (if at all) and they rely on commissioned salespeople to tell them what they need. The more insurance you pay for, the more these salespeople make. So you're often acting on advice from someone whose objective is the exact opposite of yours.

I'm not going to go into more details of insurance here because more savings tips are included in a later chapter. Suffice it to say that Sam and Sally took a closer look at their various policies and in little more than three hours found adequate coverage for about $70 a month less than they're paying now. (They saved $25 monthly on their health insurance, $35 on their car insurance, and $10 on Sam's life insurance.) That's $840 of savings a year! Not bad for three hours' work. They're now reducing their insurance expenses by $70 and increasing their Debt Destroyer by that amount.

Well, we're almost where we need to be, and that's a good thing, too, because spare money's getting pretty hard to find, and we still need $31. Let's go back to entertainment one more time. Notice that Sam and Sally list "on-line computer services" as part of their entertainment expenses. Turns out that they subscribe to

America Online to the tune of $21.95 a month. Interesting, especially since you can now get free Internet access from several different high-quality providers in exchange for having a few ads on the page. Bye-bye, AOL! The entertainment amount drops again, the Debt Destroyer goes up again, and now we need less than $10 to reach our Debt Destroyer goal.

To find that last $9.05, I asked Sam and Sally to lower their "other stuff" expenses amount by that much and try to find a few more ways to save money by checking out the extensive list of money-saving ideas in a later chapter of this book. I knew that with just a casual glance, they'd easily find a way to save much more than that.

Keep in mind that as Sam and Sally went through their spending patterns to build their $417 Debt Destroyer, the objective was to make changes in their expenditures *without damaging their lifestyle*. They still have basically the same life, with very few, if any, sacrifices. True, they did have to think a bit to consider what was worth keeping and what was worth changing, but all in all it was a pretty painless process. They haven't given up anything that they thought was really important, so they can feel pretty good about sticking to their plan. And they're going to feel even better when they see how their Debt Destroyer is about to change their future.

Before we see what will happen with Sam and Sally, let's revisit their worksheet to see how the changes we made to their spending plan showed up. Then it will be time for you to start this process yourself to see how you can build your own Debt Destroyer!

Creating Your Debt Destroyer

SAM AND SALLY SAMPLE'S FINAL SPENDING PLAN

MONTHLY EXPENSE	OLD PLAN	NEW PLAN	NOTES
Bill payments	$1,393	$1,393	
Savings	$250	$150	$100 to Debt Destroyer
Eating out	$190	$140	$50 to Debt Destroyer
Entertainment	$220	$116	$37 from health club, $25 from books, CDs, etc., $20 from premium cable, $22 from on-line services, to Debt Destroyer
Groceries	$300	$266	$34 to Debt Destroyer
Clothes	$100	$100	
Utilities	$140	$140	
Real estate taxes	$60	$60	
Home insurance	$30	$30	
Health insurance	$100	$75	$25 to Debt Destroyer
Life insurance	$50	$40	$10 to Debt Destroyer
Child care	$140	$140	
Transportation	$100	$100	
Home maintenance	$40	$40	
Charity	$50	$0	$50 to Debt Destroyer

MONTHLY EXPENSE	OLD PLAN	NEW PLAN	NOTES
Other stuff	$100	$91	$9 to Debt Destroyer
Car insurance	$92	$57	$35 to Debt Destroyer
Emergency spending	$100	$100	
Debt Destroyer	0	$417	
Total	**$3,455**	**$3,455**	

Now, one thing you might notice looking at Sam and Sally's final plan is that we're still bumping up against what's possible given their take-home pay. Depending on how much they have withheld in taxes, we may be spending more than they can afford. If that's the case, we'll have to find additional ways to save money so we can stay on track. The last thing we need is to have a plan that won't work. But there are still lots of things we can do to save money, so if we need to, we'll simply go back and adjust the plan more. We won't know until we try.

But here we are. It's been tedious, but now we've armed Sam and Sally with a powerful weapon to change everything. It's going to take the debt out of their life, and when it does, something magic is going to start to occur. Their anxiety about the future is going to fade, and it's going to be replaced with hope—even excitement! Because almost immediately Sam and Sally are going to be able to paint a new vision for themselves. One where Sam will have the ability to do what he wants to do instead of what he has to do. One where Sally can open her own seashell shop if she chooses. One where Samantha can go to college without struggling. In other words, a life of freedom to choose!

KEY POINTS FROM CHAPTER 7

→ Compute your Debt Destroyer: it's 10 percent of your monthly gross income.

→ Where's your money going? Keep track of it for a month and find out.

→ Create a spending plan. Don't forget to plan for irregular and emergency expenses!

→ When you see where your money is going, set priorities. Make a line item in your spending plan for your Debt Destroyer, and build it by taking money away from expense items you can live without.

→ Find the money for your Debt Destroyer without compromising your life. Some of the money you're spending now is worth it. But some isn't. Take the time to think about how you can find the money for your Debt Destroyer painlessly.

CHAPTER EIGHT

Wiping Out Your Debts

If you've followed Sam and Sally, you're ready to move along to step four: paying off your debts. This is the part of the program where things start to get a little more fun, because here's where we start to take control of our debts instead of allowing them to control us. Now we're actually going to see exactly how long it will take to become financially free.

Sam and Sally Sample have stopped creating more debt, they've listed and ranked their debts, they've built a $417 Debt Destroyer, and now they've ready to aim it at the first debt on their list: Sam's car loan. To refresh your memory, Sam's car loan has a $7,500 balance and payments of $212 a month. When he took out the loan about a year and a half ago, it started at $10,000 and it has an interest rate of 10 percent. So far, Sam's paid about $1,328 in interest, and if he kept paying off this loan by making the minimum monthly payment, he'd pay a total of $2,748 in interest by the time he makes the last payment on this five-year loan. But as of now, Sam's not going to be making minimum payments. He's going to start paying $629 every month (his regular payment of $212 plus the Debt Destroyer of $417). And the result? Instead of another three and a half years of payments, the car will be paid for in a little over a year. Instead of paying another $1,400 in interest, he'll pay only $400. He'll own his car outright and be one step closer to financial freedom!

Now let's assume Sam's car loan is paid off and focus our attention on the next debt on the list, Sam and Sally's credit cards. Both rank as number two on the priority list, so either could go next. But since Sam got to pay off his car, they agree that now it's Sally's turn to feel the power of the Debt Destroyer, which is about to get even more powerful! Because now it's also going to include the money that used to go to Sam's car payment.

Sally stopped using her credit card and has been making minimum monthly payments while Sam's car loan got paid off. When we started the program, Sally's MasterCard had a balance of $1,845. Her interest rate is 15 percent, and minimum payments are 2 percent per month or $10, whatever's more. When we started, Sally's minimum payment on her credit card was $37. We'll assume that that's the amount she continued to pay while Sam slaughtered the car loan. So now, one year later, Sally's current balance on this card is $1,682. (She's made twelve payments of $37 each, or $444; $163 has gone to reducing the amount she owes, and $281 has evaporated in interest.) But that $37 monthly payment is about to take off, because to that we're going to add the amount of Sam's dead car loan payment ($212) and the Debt Destroyer ($417). So now, instead of $37, Sally's going to be sending checks every month for $666 ($37 plus $212 plus $417). How long will it take to pay off her $1,682 balance? Less than three months! (To be exact, she'll send in two payments of $666 and a final payment of $388.)

In case it hasn't hit home yet, what you just read is amazing. Before we started this program, Sally was making minimum payments on her credit card. Had she continued on that path, she would have taken 253 months (21 years) to pay off that card. In the process she would also have paid $2,531 in interest. Now, thanks to the Debt Destroyer, she paid it off in 15 months and paid only another $327 in interest. Needless to say, Sam and Sally are pretty excited about the results thus far. It's been only a little more than a year, but they can already see the light at the end of the tunnel. They're really looking forward to wiping out each and every debt they have. And next to go? Sam's credit card.

Sam started the program with $2,239 on his Visa card. He was making minimum payments, which, when the program began, were $45. Like Sally, he froze that amount and kept paying it while they targeted his car loan and Sally's MasterCard. So fifteen months have gone by, and he's paid $675 more (15 times $45) on his Visa. That reduced his balance from $2,239 to $1,961. If Sam stays on his old pay-the-minimum system, he will make payments for another 279 months (23 years) and pay $3,188 more in interest along the way. But what's going to happen now? Well, let's see. The payment that Sam will be sending in every month will be the total of the payments on the car loan ($212), Sally's Master-Card ($37), his normal Visa payment ($45), plus the Debt Destroyer ($417). Grand total: $711. How long will it take to pay off his balance? Again, three months! (And again, as in Sally's case, it's really less than three months. Two payments of $711, but the third month will only be $595.) He'll pay only $56 of interest.

Okay, here we are, eighteen months into the program, and Sam and Sally have wiped out about $11,500 of their debts—debts that, had they stayed with the minimum payment trap, would have taken them decades to pay. They've also saved about $6,600 in interest.

Now let's focus on the next debt on our list, Sally's student loan. When we first met Sally, she owed $11,700 on this loan. It's an 8 percent interest rate, with payments of $182 per month. Since she's been making her regular payments, her balance has shrunk over the last eighteen months to about $9,700. How much will we start paying on this loan? Let's add it up. The total of all the old payments, plus the Debt Destroyer, came to $711. Adding the normal monthly $182 payment for this loan will make a new amount of $893. So that's how much Sally starts sending in. And when she does, she'll find that her student loan is totally wiped out in less than a year! (Eleven months, to be exact. But the last payment in this case is more than the normal $893. It's $1,171.) Instead of paying on this loan for another five years and paying another $2,400 in interest, Sally's paying for less than one year and paying only about $400 in interest.

Let's pause here once again and recap. Sam and Sally have been using a simple spending plan and the Debt Destroyer now for twenty-nine months: a little less than two and a half years. *They have now eliminated every single debt they have with the exception of their mortgage.* But let's ignore the mortgage for a moment. Had they continued to pay all their other debts by making minimum payments on each one, they would have ultimately paid about $14,000 in interest. Using this program, they've paid about $900. Had they paid only the minimum, they would have been paying the car loan for another few years, the credit cards for twenty, and Sally's student loan for more than five additional years. *With the Debt Destroyer they have no debts, other than their mortgage, after less than three years.*

Suppose Sam and Sally decide to stop right here and not even attempt to pay off their mortgage. Their debt payments have dropped from $1,393 to $917. More important, they're now used to dropping an $893 check in the mail every month. But instead of using that money to pay off debts, they get to decide to send it in to a mutual fund company instead and build up some savings. How much would they have? Well, if they earn 12 percent on that money, they'll have about $67,000 in five years, $170,000 in ten years, and $577,000 in twenty years! Not a bad nest egg for a couple who will then be in their mid- to late forties. Especially when you compare it to what they would have had under their old system—zilch, except for the money that Sam would have had in his 401(k) plan and Sally in her savings account.

Okay, enough fantasizing. Let's continue with our Debt Destroyer program for Sam and Sally and see what happens. We've got only one debt left, and that's their mortgage. Here are the details. When Sam and Sally started using this system, their mortgage was four years old, with a balance of about $120,000. It's an 8 percent, thirty-year mortgage, and the payments (principal and interest) are $917 a month. During the two and a half years that they've been paying off their other debts, they've obviously been making regular minimum payments on the mortgage. As a result, it's shrunk to about $116,500. (By the way, they've also already paid about $62,000 in interest since they borrowed this money.) If they continue to make their regular minimum payments, they're going to be paying on this mortgage for another twenty-three years, and they're going to be paying another $142,000 in interest. But they're not going to do that. Instead, they're going to combine that normal $917 payment with the total of their old payments and Debt Destroyer ($893) and start sending in $1,810 every month. How fast will their mortgage be paid off? In about seven more years. They'll still end up paying $36,000 more in interest, but that's a lot less than the $142,000 they would have paid.

So now we're done. It's been about nine and a half years, but Sam and Sally have zero debt. And they're one of a very few young couples that own their home free and clear. In the next chapter, we'll talk about what they're going to be able to do with that money as they follow the final step, investing the total of their

Debt Destroyer and their old monthly payments. But before we go on to new things, let's look at a couple of other options Sam and Sally could have chosen to pay off their debts. For example, suppose Sam and Sally decided that they were willing to embark on this debt-destroying program but agreed to do it for only five years. Well, we know that had they followed the program to the letter, after two and a half years they'd have paid all their bills with the exception of their mortgage. That would have left them another two and a half years to see what damage they could do to that giant bill. Making $1,810 monthly payments on their mortgage for two and a half years would have brought the balance down from $116,500 to $82,300. At that point, they decide to refinance their mortgage. An $82,000, thirty-year mortgage at 8 percent would require monthly principal and interest payments of about $600 per month. So even if they decided to stay with the program for just five years, their monthly bill payments would drop from nearly $1,400 per month to about $600. And while they may not be debt-free, they're pretty darn close.

The point here is that if you decide you want to stick with the program only for a certain length of time, nobody's going to come over and beat you with a baseball bat. This isn't my program; it's yours. Design it the way you want, stick with it as long as you want, and change your mind anytime you decide to. Because no matter what happens, you've still achieved something important. You've learned that the ability to live debt-free is within your grasp, and it's yours to choose whenever you want.

Okay, before we leave this chapter once and for all, let's return to the program the way it was originally mapped out and look at a brief recap of exactly what the Sample family has been able to accomplish by following it.

THE SAM AND SALLY SAMPLE SUMMARY

| DEBT | CURRENT BALANCE | OLD PAYOFF | | WITH DD | | $ SAVINGS | TIME SAVINGS |
		MONTHS	INTEREST	MONTHS	INTEREST		
Sam's Visa card	$2,239	279	$3,188	3	$56	$3,132	276
Sally's MasterCard	$1,845	253	$2,531	3	$46	$2,485	250
Sam's car loan	$7,500	42	$1,423	12	$429	$994	30
Sally's student loan	$11,700	84	$3,628	11	$401	$3,227	73
Mortgage loan	$120,000	309	$164,144	84	$36,261	$127,883	225
Totals	$143,284		$174,914		$37,193	$137,721	

This table looks a bit complicated, but it's worth understanding, so let's ponder it for a moment. When we met the Samples, they had $142,284 in debts. If we never entered their lives, and they continued to make minimum payments on those debts, the amounts in the "Old Payoff" columns would have been their story. They would have paid Sam's credit card for 279 months (about 23 years), Sally's MasterCard for 253 months (21 years), Sam's car loan for another 42 months (3½ years), Sally's student loan for another 84 months (7 years), and their mortgage loan for another 309 months (about 26 years). And they would have added a total of about $175,000 in interest to their various lenders' bottom lines. Looking at the "With DD" columns, we see that we've shortened the payoff of each debt radically and reduced the amount of interest they pay to a little over $37,000. That saves them almost $138,000 in interest!

Think about how much money that is. If you had no debts, not even a mortgage, how long could you live on $138,000? In Sam and Sally's case, when they started this program, they needed about $3,500 every month to pay their bills, but that included paying nearly $1,400 in debt payments. Without the debts, they could live just fine on only $2,100. So for them, $138,000 would allow them to retire about five and a half years earlier, ignoring inflation. They've made a choice to use that $138,000 for themselves rather than voluntarily contributing it to some company.

The money that Sam and Sally, and you, free up by paying off debts early is pretty wondrous. But what's even more important than all these numbers is something that will never show up in a table and can't be described numerically—namely, by following this program, you'll do something that's going to make you a happier, more content person. Because you're going to regain control of your life. You're going to replace a feeling of despair with one of hope. You're going to know exactly when you'll be debt-free and when you're going to be financially free. When you follow these steps, you're able to evaluate everything you do with your money and decide if what you're doing with your money is truly worth swapping your life for. You're going to feel centered and in control. You're going to feel a sense of accomplishment unique to those few individuals who establish goals and reach them, one at a time. In short, you're going to be like Sam and Sally: you're going to be glad you chose life over debt!

KEY POINTS FROM CHAPTER 8

→ Aim at the first debt on your priority list. Combine your Debt Destroyer with the monthly minimum payment and send in that amount until the first debt is paid off.

→ Move to the second debt on your list. Combine the old monthly payment from debt one, the monthly payment from debt two, and the Debt Destroyer to pay off this debt.

→ Continue down the list this way until all your debts are gone.

→ See how much interest you've saved, how much of your life you've freed up, and how much more in control you are!

CHAPTER NINE

Turning Your Debt Destroyer into a Money Machine

Once you've become free of debt, you're ready to start gaining a different kind of freedom: you know, the kind that lets you choose where to live, what to do for a living, where your kids go to college, and when and how you retire. In other words, the freedom that comes with major money in the bank. But before we start figuring out how to make it as fast as possible, let's not forget that just eliminating our debts has already made us much more free than we've ever been. Sam and Sally Sample now need one-third less money to live than they needed before, because they no longer have to pay nearly $1,400 every month to moneylenders. And should Sam want to quit working, or become unable to work, at least he won't have to worry about his family being tossed into the street. It's hard to describe the sense of freedom that you'll achieve when you don't owe anybody anything. But you'll like it, I promise!

Okay, now let's see what could happen savingswise to Sam and Sally once they follow the final step in the life-after-debt process: transforming the money that we used as a Debt Destroyer into a money machine. How? By investing it!

There's an illusion in this country that investing, particularly in the stock market, is a very complicated undertaking. Investment professionals, commercials, and the sheer volume of books and magazines on the subject convince us that this is so. We are led to believe that there are thousands of possible investments we could make, each having its own risks and rewards. And to understand these various possibilities requires years of training and expertise. Result? When we have money to invest, we are left with three choices: to pay a professional adviser to make our choices for us; to make our choices but be consumed by doubts that we've done the right thing; or the choice that most of us pick: to freeze like a deer in the headlights and do nothing. We leave our money in a bank savings account, where it is safe and simple but earns us almost nothing.

Well, let's shatter the myth that investing money is complicated. In fact, it couldn't be simpler. The concepts we need to understand to maximize our savings potential will take only a few minutes to learn and make perfect sense.

There are not thousands of ways to invest money. There are only two. Either you lend your money to someone or you become part owner of a business. In other words, you can use your savings to become either a *loaner* or an *owner*. What is the difference between the two? Well, if you're reading this book, you certainly should understand what a loaner is, because you've dealt with lots of them. When your mortgage lender loaned money to you, they looked at you as an investment. Sam and Sally's lender gave them $125,000 for a mortgage. The lender was pretty certain they'd get their money back, because they made sure Sam and Sally had enough income to pay the monthly installments. Plus, if push came to shove, they could have taken the house and sold it to get their money back. So when the lender gave Sam and Sally money, they didn't take much risk. As a result, they also didn't expect to make a huge profit when they made their investment. In Sam and Sally's case, they were happy to get 8 percent.

So how do we know when we're making a loaner type of investment? Simple—whenever we're promised our original money back and some interest for our trouble. For example, when you open a passbook account at the bank, you are loaning your money to the bank. The bank is promising you that you can have it back anytime and that, as long as you leave it there, you'll earn some interest. If you buy a bond, you are promised that when that bond comes due, you'll have your money back and some interest, too. Even a checking account is a loaner investment, although it rarely pays interest. Instead of interest, you're "earning" the convenience of being able to use checks instead of cash.

Loaner investments are very simple, and so are owner investments. When you invest money as an owner, you don't know that you'll get your money back, much less that you'll earn anything for your trouble. You're taking a lot more risk, but if you're right about the business, you could make a lot more money. Unlike loaner investments, owner investments aren't "sure things": you don't know what you're going to make, and there isn't some definite time when your money is due. When you want your money back, you simply sell your ownership to someone else, hopefully at a profit. That's exactly what you're doing when you invest in stocks. You're buying a share of someone else's business, and if that business lives up to expectations, your investment will be worth more than when you bought it.

Let's use a simple example to illustrate loaner and owner investments. Suppose your child approaches you and wants to open a lemonade stand. She's got the concept, she's willing to do the work, and she even has the stand already built. The only thing she's lacking is the $20 it will take to buy lemons, sugar, and paper cups. A loaner will say, "Okay, I'll give you the $20. But you've got to pay me back $21, and I want it within two weeks. If you don't repay me, I'll take your lemonade stand and sell it to recover my money." An owner will say, "Okay, I'll give you the $20, but I want to own one-third of the business. So if you make a profit, you'll have to give me one-third of that money. And if you sell the business, I get one-third of that money, too." If you understand that simple example, you already understand almost everything you need to know to invest your savings. You don't have thousands of choices to make, you have only two: be either a loaner or an owner. A person who invests in bonds, certificates of deposit, or a savings account is a loaner. A person who invests in stocks is an owner.

The fact is that owners always make more money over time than loaners. Why? Because they take more risk. If owners didn't make more money over time than loaners, nobody would want to be one. Capitalism needs people willing to put up money to get businesses started. And not just loaners. Loaners simply aren't willing to take the monster risk involved in lending to businesses without a proven track record. Owners are, but only because of the possibility of substantial rewards. So there's a natural balance that happens between risk and reward, owners and loaners. In our system, owners make about twice the money that loaners do. In modern times, bonds have averaged about 6 percent per year, while stocks have returned on average about 11 percent.

What you're going to do with your savings is become an owner of businesses, because that will make you the most money. In other words, you're going to invest in stocks. But you also want to minimize the risk, because ultimately the return *of* your money is more important than the return *on* your money.

How are you going to shrink the risk of being an owner? There are a few simple techniques that will help you. The first is called "diversification." Instead of investing in one business, you're going to invest in lots of businesses at the same time. You're going to spread the risk around, because you know that not all stocks will do well. Your hope is that the ones that win will more than offset the ones that lose. But how can you diversify when you don't have enough money to spread around? You're going to use mutual funds.

A mutual fund is not an investment. It's a type of account that holds investments. Think of a mutual fund as a bucket. If the bucket is filled with stocks, it's a stock mutual fund. If it's filled with bonds, it's a bond mutual fund. If it's filled with some of each, it's a balanced mutual fund. *Mutual funds were invented especially for people who want to diversify.* They allow us to own a fraction of an entire bucketful of stocks instead of just one or two. As an added bonus, they come already equipped with someone who will watch the portfolio for us, make decisions to buy or sell the individual stocks in the portfolio, and do all the paperwork. Of course, that service isn't free. There's a fee for doing all the work, but since it's spread out among all the investors in the fund, it turns out to be just a small percentage of the money we (hopefully) make on our shares.

So diversification is one way that we minimize the risk we take in becoming owners. What else can we do? Well, if you've studied investments at all, you've probably seen ads promoting investment "systems" that promise giant returns with little risk, people who say they've made 20 percent, or maybe 120 percent, every year. You send them money, and they'll share their "secrets," or they'll do the investing for you. These types of ads are almost always lies. There is no secret system that works all the time. And even if there were, why would someone who had discovered it share it with you? So when it comes to easy answers, the more outlandish the claim, the faster you should run the other way.

However, there is one investment system that actually will work for you, and it's ideal for people who can put away a little money each month. Unlike the mysterious systems you see advertised, this one is easy to understand, easy to prove, and totally free. It's called "dollar cost averaging."

Dollar cost averaging, also known as "systematic investing," is a big term for a simple idea. All you have to do is *invest a constant amount of money at fixed intervals into an investment that fluctuates in value*. This makes it perfect for us, since we have a constant amount of money to invest (the total of all of our old debt payments plus our Debt Destroyer) at a fixed interval (every month) into an investment that fluctuates in value (the stock market). Now let's look at some simple math to see why this idea works so well.

DATE	INVESTMENT	PRICE	SHARES
January	$100	$10	10
February	$100	$8	12.5
March	$100	$15	6.7
April	$100	$7	14.3
May	$100	$8	12.5
June	$100	$10	10
Totals	$600		66

Here we have an example of six months' worth of dollar cost averaging. Every month we're putting in $100 and buying a stock (or mutual fund, or bond, or gold coin—it doesn't matter) that fluctuates in price. The first month, January, the price is $10, so our $100 buys ten shares. In February, the price has fallen to $8, so our $100 buys 12.5 shares. In March, the price zooms to $15, so our $100 buys only 6.7 shares. In April, the price plummets to $7, which means our $100 buys 14.3 shares. In May, the price climbs to $8, so again we buy 12.5 shares. Then in June, with the price back at the original $10, we get another ten shares. When all is said and done, we've invested $600 and we now own sixty-six shares of stock. The stock started the year at $10, and at the end of June, it's still $10. So while there's been plenty of fluctuation in the monthly price of the stock, after six months it's still the same price it was in January. But, as if by magic, we've made money! We now own sixty-six shares of a stock that's worth $10. So our investment is worth $660. Our profit is $60, or 10 percent.

How did this happen? The magic in dollar cost averaging occurs because when prices are low, your fixed investment buys more shares. When prices are high, that same money buys fewer shares. So when an investment goes up and down in value, and ends up at the same price as it started (or higher), _you'll always make money with dollar cost averaging because your average cost is always going to be lower than the ending value._ Simple math, beautiful result.

Dollar cost averaging is custom-made for investing in the stock market and for this program. It's simple. It allows us to invest fixed amounts monthly. As you see from the example above, it's easy to prove that it works. And over time, the stock market has always gone up in value. In fact, there wasn't a single ten-year period during the twentieth century that the stock market didn't end higher than it began. So, providing we have time and discipline and are willing to tolerate some fluctuation in value, this system is perfect! In fact, dollar cost averaging offers another benefit that you may not notice at first blush—namely, that it can turn a "white knuckle" investor into a relaxed investor. Imagine for a moment that you had $100,000 to invest, and you put all that money into the stock market in one fell swoop. You know that at any moment the stock market could collapse and your nest egg could get scrambled. Think you'd be nervous? Of course. Now imagine that you're dollar cost averaging. Do you really care if the market swoons? Not only do you not care, *you actually want the stock market to fall*! Because you know that when it does, you'll be setting yourself up to make big money later by buying low now. You know that eventually, when the stock market rebounds, you'll come out smelling like a rose. So not only does dollar cost averaging work, it takes a lot of the worry out of investing in things that fluctuate in value.

Ready to leave the classroom and step out into the real world? Let's see what happens to Sam and Sally Sample when they transform their Debt Destroyer, along with their old bill payments, into a money machine. We'll assume two scenarios: one in which they earn a steady 11 percent per year and the other assuming they use dollar cost averaging in Vanguard's 500 Index Fund. This is going to bring the advantages of dollar cost averaging into sharp focus.

As you may recall, the total amount of money that Sam and Sally used to have to pay on their bills was $1,393. They also have their old Debt Destroyer of $417, for a total monthly investment of $1,810.

Scenario one: Sam and Sally invest their $1,810 every month into an investment that returns a steady 11 percent year in and year out. How much will they accumulate? Well, after five years they'll have $132,188. In ten years, they'll have $326,863. In fifteen years, they'll have $613,559. And in twenty years, they'll have $1,035,778. Not bad, but you ain't seen nothing yet!

Let's move to scenario number two: Sam and Sally invest their $1,810 every month into the index fund. Remember, this means that when share prices are low, their money buys more shares. When prices are high, they automatically buy fewer shares. We'll assume for the sake of illustration that Vanguard's 500 Index Fund performs exactly the way it did for the twenty-year period ending December 31, 2000. In five years, they'll have $231,475. In ten years, they'll have $560,254. In fifteen years, they'll have $1,361,119. And in twenty years, they'll have $3,613,956!

To be perfectly fair, let's remember that the last twenty years have been the ideal setting for dollar cost averaging, because for much of that time the stock market performed way above its normal 11 percent annual average return. And there's certainly no guarantee that what happened over the last twenty years will happen again over the next twenty. Still, when you compare $1 million to $3.5 million, that's a dramatic illustration of what dollar cost averaging (at least in the right place and at the right time) can do.

Either way, think about the implications of what we've learned here. If Sam and Sally sock away that money for twenty years, they'll be in their fifties, and whether they end up with less than $1 million or more than $3 million, they'll still be in the top 1 percent of the population in terms of income and net worth. They'll easily be able to live solely on the interest from their savings, never touching the base amount. And Samantha Sample, provided she doesn't mind living like her parents, will never have to work at all! Generations of Samples to come could live totally free of debt and the slavery that comes with it. All because Sam and Sally set out one fine day to destroy their debts.

When it's time for you to crank up your money machine, you're still going to have decisions to make. You may know, for example, that stocks are a good choice for your investment dollars and that mutual funds are a good way to own stocks. But you still have to decide which stock mutual fund to use. So here's my advice in that department: Use what I had Sam and Sally use in our dollar cost averaging example—a stock index mutual fund. These are stock mutual funds that basically attempt to mirror the return of a particular stock index.

What's a stock index? It's a list of stocks that's supposed to represent the entire market. For example, every day on your local news you hear what the Dow Jones Industrial Average did that day. You assume that you're hearing what the entire market did, but you're not. The entire stock market is made up of thousands of stocks. The Dow Jones Industrial Average is made up of only thirty stocks. It's designed to give you an idea of what the whole stock market is doing, and sometimes it does and other times it doesn't. Anyway, the Dow Jones Industrial Average is one of many stock indexes that are often quoted as a simple way of figuring out what's going on in stock land. Other common averages include the NASDAQ average, the S&P 500, and the Russell 5000 index.

Now, back to stock index mutual funds. These index funds are set up to give you the same return that you would get if you actually buy the stocks in that underlying index. One of the most common stock indexes used by these mutual funds is the S&P 500. That's an index made up of five hundred of the largest companies in the U.S. stock market. So buying an S&P 500 index mutual fund should give you about the same return as if you were actually buying shares in these five hundred big companies.

I like index funds for a couple of reasons. First, they give you a nicely diversified list of companies. Owning a bit of five hundred companies, for example, is a lot safer than owning chunks of just a few companies. Second, they don't charge a lot of money to do it. You'll recall in our discussion of mutual funds that funds charge a management fee in exchange for investing your money for you. Since they don't have lots of decisions to make when assembling index funds, mutual fund companies don't charge a hefty fee. With respect to specific funds, I've always liked the Vanguard 500 Index Fund. The Vanguard Group has traditionally charged one of the lowest management fees in the business, and they're plenty big enough to be around for a long, long time. You can reach them by calling 1-800-871-3879 or going to their Web site at www.vanguard.com. (By the way, don't think I'm getting paid to recommend Vanguard. I'm not. I just want to be as specific as possible, and they actually have a good group of mutual funds. But if you'd prefer to use another group, be my guest! It won't matter much.)

One thing that you may have to be concerned about when setting up your dollar cost averaging with mutual funds is the minimum investment required to open an account. Vanguard, for example, requires $3,000 to open an account. But then you're free to add as much or little as you'd like every month. So Sam and Sally Sample might have to hold on to their money for a couple of months until they've saved enough to start their dollar cost averaging account. No biggie. But if they don't want to wait, they don't have to, because other mutual fund groups will start them off in a systematic investing plan with as little as $50.

Before we leave this chapter, let's talk a bit about risk. We already know that stocks go up and down in value, and that's cool because that helps us make money when we use dollar cost averaging. We also know that given enough time, stocks have always done well. Remember that in any ten-year period during the 1900s, stocks always ended the period higher than they began. But I'd be a jerk if I didn't acknowledge that just because something has always happened in the past doesn't mean it will always happen in the future. It's possible that Sam and Sally will dollar cost average into stocks for years, and then, just when they're feeling free, the stock market will crash and reduce a huge amount of their savings to rubble. That's life in the stock market. It can happen. Solution? First, accept that stocks are a long-term investment. The risk of investing in the stock market is in inverse proportion to the amount of time you maintain your investments. In other words, if you're going to need your money in thirty years, you can feel pretty good that you're going to do well in the stock market. But if you're going to need your money in thirty days, what's going to happen to your savings is anybody's guess. So you never, ever want to be investing in stocks with money that you're going to need or want in the near future. If you've got a major expense coming up (say, little Samantha's college tuition or Sally's new seashell shop), you want to take that money out of harm's way well before the planned event. How? By taking it out of stocks and putting into a nice, safe (albeit boring) money market savings account.

Another thing where risk is concerned: If it doesn't feel good, don't do it. When I was a stockbroker, I used to tell my clients that there is no amount of return that justifies losing sleep. If you can't handle the roller coaster, don't ride it, no matter what anybody says and no matter what the reward. Remember, what we're aiming for here is peace of mind. Find your own mix of owner and loaner investments that makes you money but also makes you comfortable.

One last thing about investing: The more you know, the better you'll feel. Remember your first day of work? If your job requires any skill at all, you were probably totally lost when you started doing it. As time went on, your knowledge and confidence grew, and you worried less and produced more. Everything fell into place, and finally you could do your job with your eyes closed. Well, investing is the same way. It seems strange, mysterious, and confusing at first. But believe me, it isn't. Like many other vocations, it has its own vocabulary, which you have to learn. But once you've been at it for a while, you'll feel perfectly at home on Wall Street. This is a good thing, because those who are uncomfortable with what they're doing don't stick to it. And when it comes to investing, those who don't stick to it don't make money.

KEY POINTS FROM CHAPTER 9

→ Step five: Convert your Debt Destroyer into a money machine.

→ Understanding investments—it's not as hard as you think.

→ Dollar cost averaging—it works!

→ See how much you'll save.

CHAPTER TEN

205 Ways to Save

If you've gotten this far in the book, perhaps you're already out of debt. But I doubt it. It's far more likely that you're breezing through the book before you start the program to see if it will fit your situation. The idea of accelerating your debt payments to eliminate your debts is a simple one, and probably one you've already considered. But there's a major flaw in such a system, isn't there? Namely, finding the money to make it happen!

In case you don't know it, I'm a consumer reporter who appears regularly on about eighty TV stations around the country. Every week my stories reach millions of TV viewers, and over the years lots of people have called or e-mailed to tell me about their situations and ask advice. While all of these people are unique and their situations are different, most have had a couple of things in common. Their problems centered on not having enough money, and they felt they were doing the best they possibly could with the income they had. So I'm figuring odds are good that you feel the same way. I hope that reading the following pages will change your mind, and that's what this chapter is all about.

Keeping more of the money that comes into your life takes a lot more than just reading hundreds of useful savings tidbits. Each savings idea is like a little recipe to create money, but in order to follow a recipe, it helps to know how to cook first. So let's start by learning some savings fundamentals.

Savings fundamental number one: *The best way to save money is not to spend it.* And the best way not to spend money is not to buy things you don't want or need. That sounds obvious, but work with me here. Because many, if not most, of the things you spend money on now probably fall into that category. We live in a world where our "needs" are largely the figment of someone else's imagination, and that someone else works in executive suites and on Madison Avenue. In other words, what you think of as your reality may not be so real! There are fundamental physical truths, like gravity, that we know are real because we've experienced them. But we were all raised in a false societal reality created for other people's profit that has nothing to do with what's real. It's imaginary, and it's probably in direct conflict with a different, better reality that you can create simply by deciding what makes you happy and fulfilled.

Consider your basic human needs: food, clothing, and shelter. Who says that preprocessed, packaged, and "convenient" food is what you "need"? Madison Avenue invented this part of your current reality. Why? Simple. To convince you to exchange your life for some company's bottom line. The grocery store is packed with examples. Here's one: Ever heard of Breakfast Mates? I did a story on this Kellogg product a couple of years ago. Breakfast Mates is typical of convenience packaging ploys. It combines a bowl of cereal, milk, and a spoon in little single-serving containers. (What a godsend for that working mom on the run!) When I did the story, Breakfast Mates cost $1.39 per serving. Meanwhile, pouring your own cereal into your own bowl, adding your own milk, and eating it with your own spoon cost about $.29 per serving (assuming you're using the same name-brand cereal). In this case the cost of convenience was $1.10 per serving. If you've got two kids eating breakfast every day, that's $66 a month. Compounded over twenty years at 10 percent, that's more than $50,000. So that's how much our working mom is voluntarily transferring from her family to Kellogg's bottom line for the "convenience" of not having to reach for a bowl, spoon, and milk. This is just one tiny example of the way your reality is being shaped a thousand times every day when it comes to food. We all know intuitively that homemade meals made with fresh ingredients are not only better for us, they're much cheaper. And we probably all have the time to make these meals and freeze them for convenience. Isn't that a better reality? Of course. We just have to ignore Madison Avenue long enough to deprogram ourselves so we can see it.

Okay, now let's consider clothing. The reality that Madison Avenue thinks you should live in is one where fashions change constantly and your ability to appear attractive is directly related to your willingness to follow trends. But that's make-believe. The purpose of clothing is to hide your naked body while allowing you to be comfortable in extreme temperatures. Admittedly it's also true that a secondary purpose of clothing, at least in our society, is ornamental. But who says that used clothing won't satisfy these purposes? Who says that you need something that costs $200 when something that costs $50 will do the trick? Who says that something that's well cared for and ten years old isn't good enough? These aren't laws of nature. This is a reality created by a group of people who are thinking of their wealth, not yours. In my reality, which was built upon my own experiences, people who are rich often wear old clothes. People who are trying to sell something to rich people are the ones with the fancy suits.

Okay, let's consider shelter. What's wrong with living in a house that meets your needs for space and comfort? The reality that we're supposed to buy into is that we "need" to spend 25 percent of our gross monthly income on a house that's more a status symbol than a place to stay warm and dry. As a result, we have people living in giant mansions with rooms they've never visited. And those people are often unhappy because the status that comes with such a house in no way enhances their self-esteem. It does, however, significantly enhance their debt burden. Who says that a modest house that provides shelter isn't enough? This isn't a law of nature like gravity. It's invented, and it's not true. When I was a stockbroker, some of the wealthiest clients I visited lived in modest homes, often much more modest than the homes of the indebted salespeople who catered to them. Again, that's my reality, and it came from my own observation.

What I'm trying to say here is that the single best way to save money is to develop a new reality and a new attitude to go with it. Decide what really makes *you* happy, what you're willing to trade *your* life for. These things differ for everyone because everyone's idea of happiness and fulfillment is unique. But if you're about to pull out your wallet for anything that isn't truly important to *your* happiness, put your wallet away. That will not only save you a ton of cash, it will put you in control of your own life.

Savings fundamental number two is a lot more basic: When it comes to buying long-lasting stuff, *don't buy anything new that you can buy used*. We often forget that many of the things we go to the store to buy are available for much less at yard sales, in the classifieds, or at consignment shops. This not only saves you a boatload of money, it helps save the planet. I'm not suggesting you buy only used things: sometimes finding what you want used is more hassle than it's worth, or what you really want isn't available used. But there are plenty of things that you have right now that you could have bought used, resulting in a lot less debt or more savings.

Here's savings fundamental number three: When it comes to buying consumable stuff (food, toiletries, cleaning supplies, and so on), *don't buy name brands when generic substitutes are available.* Suppose you have a party, and someone peeks into your medicine cabinet and finds all generic items. Would you be embarrassed? Most of us, at least if we're being honest, would probably admit to at least a twinge of embarrassment. But why would you be ashamed of being smart? Because we've been conditioned by Madison Avenue to believe that name brands are better than generic brands. Now don't get me wrong, sometimes name brands *are* better than generic brands. But many times they're not, and we should be happy (in fact, proud) to use generics in those situations. Doing anything else is simply donating free money to people who already have plenty. And what's so smart about that?

Okay, enough with the fundamentals. Let's get on with some specific ways that you can keep more of your money to do the things that are important to you.

A note about the Net: The following list of money-saving tips is sprinkled with Internet Web site addresses. You can also visit me on-line for additional tips and information through my Web site: www.moneytalks.org. If you don't have a computer, that doesn't mean you don't have access to the Internet. You do, because you can go to the library and surf the World Wide Web anytime you want for free. Part of every local phone bill you pay goes toward providing for this service. Use it! If you are computer illiterate, it's time to educate yourself: there are just too many juicy consumer tidbits and savings techniques available in cyberspace to ignore. But if you insist on being the last person on earth to learn to use a computer, you'll still find much of the same information in traditional written form at your library. Ask your librarian to help you find it.

General Tips

1. **Pay attention to where your money is going.** Carry a little memo pad around and keep track of everything you spend. Like magic, the simple act of writing stuff down will often keep you from spending money. It also helps you to look at where your money is going and allows you to make informed decisions about how much money you really need to live the life you want.

2. **Make a simple spending plan.** You wouldn't think of setting off on a long trip without a map. A spending plan is simply a map to help guide you to where you're going financially. It allows you to set goals and evaluate your progress. There's no successful company that doesn't plan their cash outlays. Why don't you?

3. **Make sure everybody's on the bus.** Changing your spending habits is hard to do if everyone else in your life isn't reading from the same page. Make sure everyone in the family is committed to the trip before you leave the curb.

Smart Shopping

4. **Be a bargainer.** When you're buying something expensive, or buying a service, always bargain on price. It never hurts to ask, and if you're buying something big, like a TV, a refrigerator, or a computer, you might save yourself 10–20 percent.

5. **Cash is king.** Again, if you're buying something expensive, ask for a discount for using cash. Did you know that when you use a credit card, the merchant has to pay 2–4 percent to the

bank? Therefore, when you pay cash (or write a check) you're saving them that money. Ask for it!

6. **Don't buy extended warrantees.** They're a major profit item for the vendor, and 80 percent are never used. That's why they push you so hard to buy them!

7. **Don't wait till the last minute to shop.** Obviously, less time gives you less flexibility. The seasons, the start of school, birthdays, Christmas: nearly everything we shop for is pretty darn predictable.

8. **The calendar is your friend.** Consider the times of the year that retailers love most: holidays! Halloween, Valentine's Day, Christmas, and Thanksgiving are all great times to save money ... if you're willing to wait a bit. You'll often see big sales just prior to these holiday times, but those savings pale in comparison with the discounts you'll get by waiting until the days after the event. Buy next year's Halloween costume on November 1, your Christmas decorations on January 1, and so on. Want to get even better deals? Try outlet malls.

9. **Always use a list.** And don't buy anything that isn't on it. Depending on what you're shopping for, you can easily save 10–15 percent with this tip alone.

10. **Don't shop hungry.** If you're shopping for food, it'll make you buy more. If you're shopping for anything else, it'll make you hurry. Also avoid shopping depressed. Buying stuff you don't need won't make you feel better, but if you're not careful, you'll do it anyway.

11. **Shop alone.** Kids and spouses who act like kids will often whine, cajole, or otherwise try to influence you into impulse buys. Leave 'em at home.

12. **Keep receipts and send in rebate slips.** Very few consumers actually return rebate coupons. Which is, of course, exactly what the manufacturers are hoping for. Don't be a

sap ... get what you've got coming. Keep your receipts and don't hesitate to return anything that disappoints you in even the slightest way. Keep in mind that many stores will refund the difference if you find an item cheaper elsewhere after you've bought it, and most will match competitors' prices.

13. **Get 10–15 percent off by opening a department store credit account.** Stores often offer you substantial discounts to induce you to sign up for (and get hooked on) their high-interest credit cards. Fine. Take them up on their offer and get your discount. But when the statement comes in, pay the bill in full and cancel the card in writing. Don't just stop using the card: if you don't officially cancel the account, it will continue to be reflected on your credit history.

14. **Don't pay for extra features that you don't need.** Fancy extras on everything from cars to VCRs are often high-profit-margin items for manufacturers and dealers. Even if it costs only "a little more," why buy things you'll never use? Fewer gadgets can also mean longer product life with less in repair bills.

15. **Buy your furniture and appliances prescratched.** Scratch-and-dent can save you plenty, especially when you bargain down the price even more.

16. **Open your own temporary store by having a garage/ yard sale.** You probably have lots of stuff that you don't want or need, and that's money just lying around your house. Spend a day going around your home and identifying everything that you haven't touched in a year. That's stuff you should probably either sell or donate to charity. If you decide on a yard or garage sale, talk to neighbors first and see if they'll join you: the more stuff you have and the more people you have, the better off you'll be. Publicize the sale with signs around the neighborhood (providing they're legal) and a newspaper ad

several days in advance of the sale. List your best items in the ads (for example, tools and antiques are top draws). Prepare carefully for the sale. Segregate items by price ($.25 table, $.50 table, and so forth), and use colored tags to identify items. Make it simple for shoppers and for you. If you don't sell everything, that may not be all bad, because in some cases you might be better donating items to charity anyway. For example, if you're going to sell a shirt for ten cents, you might be able to donate it to Goodwill and get a one-dollar tax write-off. That could save you more in taxes than you'd have gotten from selling it for cash. When you have a sale, beware of shoplifters. Believe it or not, people will actually steal things that they could buy for a dime!

17. **Buy at yard and garage sales.** This is the smartest shopping you can do, provided you confine your purchases to what you actually need.

18. **Share the cost.** If you're going to buy something that is useful to your neighbors and is needed only occasionally, start your own "co-op." Splitting the cost of a ladder, a lawn mower, gardening equipment, tools, and many other expensive items will reduce their cost by at least half (depending on how many people are in your co-op) and will barely register on the "inconvenience scale."

19. **When clothes shopping, start at home.** Many of us go to the store and buy clothes when we already have similar items at home that we've forgotten. Do a careful inventory of your clothes before you buy anything, including the ones you have tucked away in the back of your closet or attic. Added bonus: This will allow you to make money by selling, consigning, or donating things you're never going to wear again.

Staying in Shape

20. **Walking or jogging in your neighborhood is free,** and fresh air is better than the air in a health club.
21. **Buy inexpensive workout and aerobic videotapes,** and use them at home with your TV. You could easily get a better workout than you'd get at a health club, and you can own the tapes for $5–$10 each. Rent them first until you know you like them.
22. If you insist on joining a health club, **try joining for a month or buying a series of single-day passes first** to make sure you're going to have the time and discipline to stick with it. Avoid long-term membership contracts.
23. **Avoid buying sports accessories until you know that the activity is a fixed habit.** For example, don't buy a gym bag until you've been to the gym twenty times. Don't buy good inline skates until you've racked up two hundred miles on the cheap ones. Reward yourself with a Walkman after you've jogged twenty miles with only the sound of the wind in your ears. Then buy all that stuff used.

Transportation: New Cars

24. **Avoid new cars.** Because cars are made better now than they used to be, buying used isn't as risky as it was before. Buying a car even two years old can save you from 25 percent to 40 percent. But if you are going to buy new . . .
25. **Always negotiate price, never payments.** Payments can be manipulated so that practically anything is affordable. Salespeople will always try to get you to talk payments. Good negotiators always talk price: the payments will take care of themselves. (Obviously, I hope you're not borrowing to buy, but just in case. . . .)

26. **Choose your make and model carefully.** You obviously want to buy a car that's within your price range, but don't forget to consider other costs, like insurance, gas mileage, maintenance, and repair. These numbers are available in new-car guides at your library or on-line at Web sites like www.kbb.com and www.edmunds.com.

27. **Get the dealer's invoice price before you shop.** You can find it at many Web sites (like the ones above) or in new-car guides at the library. Your objective is to pay no more than 3 percent over the invoice amount. Don't forget to get the dealer's invoice price of the options you want on your car and negotiate those, too!

28. **Just say "no" to fees.** One of the main ways dealers make money on cars is to pad prices with extra fees like "documentation," "advertising," and others. Eliminate the ones you can, understand the ones you can't, and check the final contract to make sure that eliminated fees don't magically reappear.

29. **Always get preapproved for a loan before you shop.** Even if you end up using dealer financing, it's important to know how much you can borrow and what the rates will be. That makes you a tougher negotiator. You'll especially need to know this information in order to choose between a rebate and low-interest financing. There are on-line calculators that will help you decide between a rebate and low-interest financing (do a Web search), but generally the rebate is the best option. (Especially since you're not borrowing anyway, right?)

Transportation: Used Cars

30. **Always buy used.** A two-year-old car may have depreciated in price by 50 percent, but it's still got 70 percent of its useful life left. That's why used cars are nearly always a better deal than new. Plus, the insurance cost is lower.

31. **Always be preapproved for a loan before you shop.** As with new-car shopping, you want to have all the loan details worked out before you go. That way, when you find what you're looking for, you can pounce before it gets away.

32. **Do your homework.** Check the cost of repairs, maintenance, licensing, fuel, and insurance before you decide on a make and model. Then arm yourself with the suggested retail and wholesale prices. You can find them at car Web sites (see number 26), in used-car guides at the library, or through your credit union or other lender.

33. **Check with private sellers.** Dealers offer the advantage of broader selection and, in some situations, warranties. Private sellers may offer you a better deal, however, and you also get to see who's been driving the car and how it's been kept and maintained. But the greatest advantage of private sellers is that you don't have to feel outclassed, saleswise.

34. **Make friends with a mechanic or two.** Mechanics often hear of people who want to sell their car. They can not only help you find a great car at a great price, but they can sometimes vouch for the condition of the car.

35. **Don't think of buying a used car without a thorough inspection.** Even if your car of choice was driven only to church on Sundays, have it thoroughly inspected by a qualified mechanic before you think of buying it. This can not only help you avoid a nightmare, it could help you negotiate a better price.

Transportation: Leasing Cars

36. **Leasing is more complicated than buying** and since it's really borrowing, I hope you don't ever do it. But if you're going to anyway, remember: Leasing is essentially like financing part of a car's life. There are three main components to a lease: the

capitalized cost ("purchase" price), the money factor (interest rate), and the residual value (what it's worth when the lease is up). You should be familiar with each of these terms, because changing any one of them will change the lease payments. And when you approach leasing, ignore payments. Negotiate the capitalized cost just as you would if you were buying, then the money factor just as you would if you were borrowing. Let the payments take care of themselves.

37. **Be aware of the fees for excess mileage and excess wear and tear.** They should show up in microscopic print somewhere in the contract. Understand them, and realize that average lease return fees total more than $1,000. Think about that before you lease.

38. **Whether you're buying or leasing, negotiate the value of your trade-in before you negotiate the new car.** Actually, you should never trade in a used car. You're nearly always better off selling it yourself. But if you are going to trade in your old car, establish its value before you start on the new-car purchase. The dealer will want to make it a part of the new-car transaction. It isn't.

Transportation: Repair, Maintenance, and So Forth

39. **Always use the lowest-octane gas your owner's manual suggests.** While only 15 percent of cars require premium, 25 percent of gasoline sold is premium. Why? Probably because some people respond to advertising instead of reading their owner's manual.

40. **Keep your car tuned and check your tires.** These simple things can easily save you $100 per year in gas, as well as provide giant increases in your engine and tire life.

41. **Carpool!** Sharing the ride with just one other person will cut

your commuting costs in half. You'll also reduce your stress level by 50 percent.

42. **Keep your air and fuel filters clean.** Your car will perform better, your mileage will increase, and your engine will last longer. Best of all, these items are inexpensive.

43. **Make it a habit to be a smooth operator.** Scan the road ahead and try to anticipate any slowdowns. Try to maintain as constant a speed as possible. That will save gas and make you a safer driver.

44. **Lighten up.** Roof racks hurt mileage by spoiling your aerodynamics. If you don't use 'em, lose 'em. To increase your mileage even more, take the excess weight out of your car.

45. **Get a good mechanic.** The best way to save money on cars is to keep yours as long as possible, and the best way to do that is to have it serviced well and regularly. To find a good mechanic, try calling some classified ads placed by people selling cars similar to yours. They might have a good suggestion. In most cities, you can also check with AAA, even if you're not a member. At the minimum, find a mechanic who's certified and experienced with your type of car. Always get estimates in writing before work is done, and always get used parts back.

46. **If they'll work as well, try used or rebuilt parts.** Your mechanic or body shop will know if OEM (original equipment manufacturer) parts are necessary or desirable. If they are, fine. But if they're not, you can save a bundle.

47. **Shop rental cars!** If you're going to rent a car, comparison-shop heavily. Prices differ a bunch depending on company, current demand, and location. Don't hesitate to pit companies against each other. And ask as many times as possible about special deals, promotions, coupons, and any source of potential savings such as membership in AARP or AAA. Even while you're standing at the counter waiting for your reserved car,

it's not too late to ask for a discount or free upgrade. Sometimes a smile and a simple request will do wonders.

48. **Don't buy rental car insurance if you can avoid it.** This policy ranks high among the Western world's great rip-offs. Your regular car insurance or possibly even your gold credit card will often render it unnecessary. Check before you leave home.

49. **Keep change in your car.** How many times have you not fed a parking meter because you couldn't find any change? Keep some in your car at all times and avoid unnecessary tickets.

50. **Make travel less taxing.** Keep a little notebook in your car so you can record the mileage you log on deductible trips. Trips to the doctor, job-hunting trips, trips for charity—all deductible, which means you could be on the road to lower taxes.

Insurance

51. **Consider consolidation.** Some insurance companies offer substantial discounts for insuring both your home and car. See if yours does.

52. **Raise your deductibles.** The easiest and fastest way to lower insurance bills is to raise deductibles. Going from a $250 to a $1,000 deductible can reduce your home or car coverage cost by 20 percent and takes only about three minutes.

53. **Don't buy credit life.** These are gimmick policies that are basically life insurance tied to specific debts, like a credit card or mortgage. Regular term life insurance is a much less expensive alternative.

54. **Don't buy whole life insurance.** Whole life or permanent life insurance combines an insurance policy with an investment account. Unless you're rich and need a permanent policy to help pay estate taxes, it's generally a better idea

to buy cheaper term coverage and do your own investing separately.

55. **Don't insure your child's life.** The purpose of life insurance is to replace the earnings of a key breadwinner in the event of untimely death. While the death of a child is certainly a tragedy, it's rarely a financial calamity. There are better investments you can make for a child.

56. **Shop your coverage.** Whatever type of insurance you have, you should shop it every six months. This is a competitive business and getting more so all the time. So pull out those policies and make sure you're getting the best deal.

57. **Cancel your car coverage!** This may seem like a strange idea, but if the cost of your annual comprehensive/collision coverage is more than 10 percent of the value of your car, you could consider dropping it. (Obviously you should never under any circumstances drive without liability.) For example, if you're paying $500 in comp/collision premiums to cover a car that's worth only $5,000, you're at the 10 percent threshold. If the potential loss of $5,000 worth of car is worth not spending $500 every year, consider dropping the coverage. This is an option only if you don't have a loan on the car, since lenders require you to maintain full coverage to protect their collateral.

58. **Flaunt your good driving record.** If you've had no accidents or tickets during the last three years, make sure your rates reflect that. Most insurance companies don't automatically lower your premiums when old citations fall away. You have to call and make them reduce your bill.

59. **Get what's coming to you!** Keep the following list of possible discounts available, and ask for them all when you get car insurance quotes (many might be applicable to homeowners as well): accident-free, multiple cars, short mileage (usually less than 7,500 miles per year), good student, absent student (if

your kid is away at school without the car, they might reduce your family rate), over fifty, graduate of defensive driving course, nonsmoker, air bags, antilock brakes, automatic seat belts, and antitheft devices. Any of these possible discounts could save you money. And when you're done reciting them to the insurance company, be sure to ask, "Did I leave anything out? Do you have any other ways for me to save money?"

60. **If you're changing policies,** make sure your new one is in effect before you drop your old one. This applies to every kind of coverage: health, life, homeowners, and automotive.

61. **Get rid of PMI ASAP.** Private mortgage insurance (PMI) is normally required if you have less than 20 percent equity in your home. And it can easily cost $50 a month. As soon as you're sure you've got the magic 20 percent, whether it's by appreciation or paying off mortgage principal, call your lender and tell them you want out of PMI. Expect them to make you jump through hoops since they make tons of money from this coverage.

62. **If you're going to buy travel insurance,** make sure you get only coverages you need, like trip cancellation coverage. Policies insuring your luggage are normally so riddled with exceptions that they're virtually useless.

63. **Don't buy specialty insurance,** like cancer coverage. Put your money into a good general health insurance policy instead.

64. **Keep health insurers honest.** If you're like most people, you pay no attention to your health coverage. So when your insurer messes up, which they frequently do, you don't know it. For example, many policies have a deductible of $200 per person, $400 per family. But are you keeping track of when you reach those magic numbers? Don't assume your insurance company is. Read and understand your policies and keep your own tally: you may need it for tax purposes anyway.

65. **Don't let your doctor cost you money.** If your health

insurance provider agrees to pay 80 percent of covered procedures, that generally means they'll pay 80 percent of what they think is reasonable for that procedure, not 80 percent of whatever it costs. So find out what your insurance company is willing to pay and if your doctor can do it for that amount.

66. **HMOs are normally the cheapest way to get health coverage.** In the world of health, choosing your own doctors is an expensive alternative.

Banking

67. **Shop your banking services carefully.** As banks consolidate, competition is decreasing and fees are increasing. Think about the services you need first, then call around and see who can deliver them for the least money. Do you do a lot of ATM transactions? Then you need a bank with lots of branches and ATM machines to avoid paying "foreign" ATM fees. Do you travel a lot? Then you want a bank with branches in the states you often visit. Do you need on-line banking? Find a bank that doesn't charge for this convenience. Do you write just a few checks a month? Find a bank with a stripped-down, inexpensive checking account. You get the picture. Think about what you need before you go shopping, and be sure you understand all the fees before you sign up. In general, you're going to get better deals from smaller local banks than from the biggies.

68. **Don't use a bank!** Instead, use a credit union. Credit unions generally offer lower rates on loans, higher rates on savings, and lower fees than commercial banks. To find one that will accept you as a member, ask your employer or open the Yellow Pages and make a few calls.

69. **Use only your bank's ATM.** Avoid fees to get to your own money.

70. **Don't use a passbook savings account.** These accounts are old-fashioned and pay very little interest. You're much better off with your bank's money market account. You'll earn more interest, your money will be just as safe, and you'll still be able to get to it at any time. For a little more interest with just a bit more risk, consider money market mutual funds. These aren't federally insured like bank money markets, but they're normally plenty safe.

71. **Check your checks!** There's no law that says you have to buy checks and deposit slips from your bank. There are companies that will sell them to you for 50 percent less.

72. **Don't pay fees to have a checking account.** There are now on-line banks that will charge you nothing for your checking account and even pay interest on it. Shop around and you might even find the same with old-fashioned bricks-and-mortar banks. Eliminating the fee on your checking account could easily save you $100 a year.

73. **Be aware of fee changes.** Did you know that banks most often mail notices of fee increases between Thanksgiving and Christmas? That's because they know that you're least likely to read them during that busy time. Don't let them fool you. Read fee notices.

74. **Ask and you might receive.** Years ago, *Money* magazine called ten credit card lenders and merely asked them to lower their interest rates. Three out of ten did it! This could work in all areas of banking. If your bank is charging you high interest or high fees, try saying something like "Gee, I've banked here for years, but I can get much better deals from your competitors. Can't you lower [eliminate?] this fee [interest rate] so I don't have to leave you?" You'd be surprised how often this simple tactic will work.

75. **Go direct.** Direct deposit of money you receive and direct payment of bills you owe can save you postage, gas, and hassle.

And it could increase your interest earnings to boot. See what your bank offers and take advantage of it.

76. **Balance your checking account.** Estimates of people who don't bother to reconcile their checking accounts range from 6 percent to 20 percent. If you don't keep track of what's in your account, you should just carry cash. Because sooner or later you're going to be paying giant fees for bounced checks.

77. **Give yourself credit.** If you're going to have credit cards, in spite of my advice, get the best possible deals. If you pay off your balance every month, get a card with no fee. If you don't, get the lowest possible interest rate, but don't forget to include any annual fees in the interest price you're paying. You can find good credit card deals in magazines like *Money* and *Kiplinger*, or on-line at Web sites like www.bankrate.com and www.ramresearch.com. And, as you've learned from reading this book, remember that a life with no debt is always your best option.

78. **Be aware of "stealth" fees.** Hidden fees abound in credit cards. They include fees for going over your credit limit, transferring your balance to another company, and paying late. The only way you have of finding out about these fees is to call the issuer or read the microscopic print found on the original disclosure paperwork or monthly statements. You should also be aware that your card issuer can sell your account at any time to a company that will change every term you have, including the interest rate. Be vigilant.

79. **Know the lingo.** When we shop for credit cards (or any loans, for that matter), the focus is always on the interest rate we're being charged. While that's obviously the main thing, it's not the only thing. In the case of credit cards, you also need to inquire about the "grace period." That's the period of time you have after using the card before the interest clock starts tick-

ing. Twenty-one days is typical, but obviously the longer the better. You also need to know about all fees: the annual fee and any possible fees that could occur on cash advances, late payments, and balance transfers. Only when you've uncovered all the costs can you really compare apples to apples.

Investing

80. **Join your employer's voluntary retirement plan, especially if it offers a match.** After your debts are paid off, saving through a retirement plan has some great advantages, like investing automatically and being able to defer taxes on the money you make. Even before you pay off your debts, you should enroll in a plan and deposit enough to get the full match from your employer. If your employer is offering a 50 percent match, that's like earning 50 percent on your money with no risk! That's a deal that's hard to beat.

81. **Don't buy load mutual funds.** A "load" refers to a commission, and there's no reason for you to ever pay one. If you're buying a mutual fund through a financial adviser of any kind (except ones you pay by the hour), you're undoubtedly going to pay a load. Do your own research, buy your own funds, and don't pay a commission.

82. **Buy stocks direct, then DRIP by DRIP.** You can buy nearly one thousand different stocks by going direct to the company that issues them. While the fees charged for doing this vary from company to company, they are often much less than the fees you'd pay by going through a broker. DRIPs ("dividend reinvestment plans") allow you to reinvest quarterly stock dividends into additional shares of stock. There is normally no fee for this service. To find out if the company you're interested in offers a DRIP or direct investment plan, call the

company's investor relations number and ask. To get a company's investor relations phone number, either you can go to the Web site of any on-line brokerage firm (try www .etrade.com) and look up company research or you can go to your public library and look in investment guides (try _Value Line_). There are also Web sites that, for a small fee, will help you establish direct investment and DRIP accounts. One example is www.directinvest.com.

Real Estate

83. **Time your home purchase.** The hardest months to sell a house are the best months to buy one: October, November, and December.

84. **Sell it yourself.** Real estate commissions are among the costliest of fees, especially considering the value you get in return. If you're in a lousy housing market, you may not have a choice: Realtors will expose your home to the maximum number of potential buyers. But if the market's popping, try selling it yourself, after reading a book or two on the subject. Many other people have gone this way successfully, and it's a way to save many thousands of dollars.

85. **Buy direct from sellers.** People who sell their homes themselves are saving money on real estate commissions. They should be able to sell for less. But doing things without Realtors also means more education for you. So be knowledgeable before you try bringing home the savings.

86. **Don't even think of buying a house until you've had it thoroughly inspected.** Not only will you be more comfortable with the purchase, but you can use the report as leverage to get the price lowered. (The inspector will _always_ find something wrong.)

87. **Negotiate rent.** For some reason, everybody knows they're supposed to negotiate house purchases, but almost nobody thinks of negotiating rent. Why should you pay the same rent as the punk rockers upstairs? You're a quiet, high-quality, self-sufficient tenant who will be less hassle than other people. Therefore you should pay less rent. (Trust me, as a former landlord, this is absolutely true.) Another technique that may help you negotiate lower rent is to offer to pay several months up front. These ideas may not work, but it costs nothing to try.

Energy Savings

88. **Get a free energy audit.** Many utility companies will come out to your house for free or at a nominal cost and tell you how to save money. If yours will, let 'em. And while they're there, ask if they have any off-peak, load-management, or other savings programs.

89. **Here's a bright idea.** Fluorescent bulbs use 75 percent less energy than incandescent and last up to ten times longer. Use as many as you can. And for nonreading lights, lower the wattage of your bulbs.

90. **Run your dishwasher less.** One less time per week can save you $50 per year. Air-drying your dishes will also save money.

91. **Buy energy-efficient appliances.** Those yellow energy guide stickers are important reading, especially if you're shopping for a refrigerator, air-conditioning, or a furnace.

92. **Change your filters.** Keeping your furnace and air-conditioning filters like new can save you up to 10 percent per month on costs. Don't check them once a year, check them once a month.

93. **Seal it up.** Use a lighted candle to detect air leaks around doors and windows. Caulk is much cheaper than electricity.

94. **Dial for dollars.** Turning your thermostat dial up or down by just one degree can reduce your energy bill by up to 5 percent per month.

95. **Use ceiling fans.** Ceiling fans cost less than one-tenth of what air conditioners cost to run. In the winter, reverse the blade direction to force warm air down from the ceiling.

96. **Insulate.** Adding insulation can reduce cooling and heating costs by up to 20 percent. Some utility companies even offer rebates to help defray the cost, and the cost isn't that much anyway. You can add insulation to a 1,500-square-foot home for about $200. Extra insulation in the attic can easily pay for itself in a few years.

97. **Try a heat pump.** While they may not be the perfect solution for all parts of the country, a heat pump can reduce your power bills by 40 percent.

98. **Be careful with vent fans.** Believe it or not, a kitchen or bath ventilation fan can completely empty a house of warm or cool air in about an hour. Use them, then turn them off.

99. **Use your drapes.** In the winter, open your south-facing drapes during the day to capture heat, then close them at night to keep it in. Do the opposite in the summer.

100. **Beware portable heaters.** Using a portable heater costs close to $.09 per hour. So using one eight hours per day will cost about $5 a week, or $20 per month.

101. **Pay attention to the temperature.** An indoor/outdoor thermometer can tell you when to open and close your windows and doors.

102. **Close off rooms you're not using, but be careful about closing vents.** Closing too many vents can reduce the efficiency of your heating and cooling. This is especially true for heat pumps.

103. **Be a stripper.** Weather-strip all your doors and windows.

104. **Cover yourself.** An electric blanket costs only a little over a penny per hour to operate. Buy one cheap at a yard sale.

105. **Go for the juice.** A 220-volt air conditioner is cheaper to run than a 120-volt.

106. **Use turbines.** Turbine fans on the roof will let out summer heat, but be sure to cover them in the winter.

107. **Stay out of hot water.** You can buy a water heater blanket for about $15 that will save you about $50 per year. And while you're at it, insulate the pipes as well. If you can set your water heater to be used only at certain times of the day and turned off at night, you can save $20 per month.

108. **Don't be a drip.** Leaky faucets are a problem, but leaking hot water is an emergency. Hot-water drips can cost you $25 per month!

109. **Grow some savings.** A tree planted on the south side of your house can provide shade in the summer. Don't plant an evergreen, though: you want those leaves gone in the winter.

110. **Turn off your furnace pilot light in the summer.** You can also save by turning off your stove's pilot light and using a lighter.

111. **Use your fireplace.** Wood is still usually cheaper than gas. But be sure to close your flue tightly when you're not using it, and make sure the fit is snug. Caulk around the hearth. If you don't use your fireplace at all, plug and seal your chimney flue.

112. **Dress for success.** Don't try to stay dressed in shorts all winter long. Wear clothing appropriate to the season, and adjust your thermostat accordingly.

113. **Put your water on restriction.** Low-flow shower heads can save a family up to $200 per year by reducing water flow by up to 50 percent.

114. **Water early.** Try to water between six and eight A.M. That minimizes evaporation.

115. **Don't waste water.** You don't need to run the water while you're shaving or brushing your teeth.

116. **Save a load.** Every load of wash uses between twenty-five and fifty gallons of water. The same is true of your dishwasher. And you shouldn't need to soak or prewash dishes unless the food is burned or otherwise stuck on. By the way, the amount of detergent you use for both clothes and dishwashing could probably be reduced. Try using three-quarters of the amount recommended.

117. **Go out back and hang out.** If you've got a decent-size family, hanging your clothes out to dry can save you $40 a month in electricity.

118. **Be cool.** Using cold water only can save you 90 percent of the cost of washing your clothes. Disconnect the hot-water hose.

119. **Refrigerator etiquette.** If you're buying a new refrigerator, remember that top-mounted freezers are cheaper to operate than side-by-sides, and don't buy more refrigerator than you need. Automatic ice makers add about $200 to the initial cost of a refrigerator, cost about $50 a year to operate, and are the first thing to break. If your refrigerator is old, check the seal by putting a dollar bill in the door. If it falls out, replace the seal. See that the cooling coils in the back are clean. And avoid repeated opening of your refrigerator door. When you're getting ready to cook or cleaning up after a meal, make it a game to see if you can open the refrigerator door only once.

120. **Oven etiquette.** Use energy-saving appliances like microwaves, pressure cookers, and toaster ovens instead of always using the oven or stove. You can buy 'em cheap at yard sales. Turn off your electric burner three minutes before the rice or pasta recipe calls for: it'll stay hot that long. Same with your oven. And if you are going to bake in the oven, why not throw in an extra potato or two for tomorrow's casserole?

Telephone Savings

121. **Use the Internet!** E-mail is free. Long-distance calling isn't (unless you also do that on the Internet). The Internet is also a great free way to find numbers instead of using directory assistance. But if you are going to use directory assistance, your local one (411) is almost always cheaper than the national ones you see advertised on TV.

122. **Stop leasing.** You'll usually save money by buying your own phones.

123. **Hang up on frills.** The phone company is a master at getting us to buy services. They sell your phone number to telemarketers, then sell you caller ID to thwart them. In round two, they sell to telemarketers services that block caller ID, then sell you a gadget that won't allow blocked calls to ring through. Don't play this ongoing game. Get the basic package, skip the frills, and save yourself $100 or more per year.

124. **Turn the tables on telemarketers.** One of the most popular TV news stories I've ever done involves changing from victim to predator in the cold-calling jungle. Here's how it works. Federal law requires that almost anyone who solicits you by phone give you their name *and* either address or phone number (which they virtually never do). The law also requires that they call between the hours of eight A.M. and nine P.M. And if you ask to be put on their "do not call" list, nobody from that company is allowed to call you for ten years. Finally, they're required to furnish you with their written "do not call" policy upon request. Now, here's the cool part. Companies are allowed one mistake per year, then they are subject to a $500 fine per violation. So here's what you do: Keep a pad and pencil by the phone. When you're cold-called, ask to be put on the "do not call" list and ask for a copy of their written policy. Make a note of the date, time, and person you talked

to. If that company contacts you again, let them know you're supposed to be on their "do not call" list. That was their one allowable mistake. If they call you again, get their address, because you're about to make some money. Send a letter to the company threatening to sue them in your local small claims court for $500 per offense because the company is in violation of the Telephone Consumer Protection Act. More than likely, the company will offer you a check ($250–$300) to avoid the hassle of a court hearing that they're going to lose. Believe it or not, informed Americans have already collected hundreds of thousands of dollars with this strategy (and no doubt had fun doing it!). That's just the gist of what you need to know, however; to learn more, go to www.junkbusters .com. Sites like this can also help you reduce your junk mail.

125. **Shop your long distance.** Internet sites like www.trac.org and www.abelltolls.com can help you find the best long-distance calling plan for your needs. If you don't have Internet access, go to the library. Remember, part of your monthly phone bill goes to pay for library Internet access, so use it! Even if you aren't willing to go to the hassle of finding the best long-distance deals, at least call your current long-distance provider and make sure you're on the cheapest plan for your needs. Before you start shopping for long distance, be sure to look at a few bills to see what your calling patterns are. Do you make most of your calls to one person? Mostly at night and on weekends? How long are your average calls? How much do you typically spend? This type of information is important to know before you can find the best overall plan for your family. And, just as with other services, don't be afraid to ask for a discount. The way to do it is simply to say you've found a better deal elsewhere and ask your current company to match the rates. Don't lie, however: they're likely to verify the information.

126. **Know the lingo.** It's hard to shop smart for something when you don't know what questions to ask. In long-distance land, there are three major ones. First, "What is your cost per minute?" Second, "What is your billing increment?" Billing increment is crucial if you make lots of calls, especially lots of short calls. Billing increments for the "big three," AT&T, Sprint, and MCI/WorldCom, are typically one minute. That means if you talk for one minute and one second, you get charged for two minutes. Other companies may have billing increments of only six seconds, which is obviously a better deal. Third question: "What fees will I pay?" Many of the larger companies charge a fixed monthly fee in addition to their rate per minute. Depending on what you're spending, this seemingly small fee could radically change your cost per minute.

127. **Don't take their word for it.** We tend to regard anything printed out by a computer as accurate, which is often far from the case. Look at your bills and make sure you're actually paying the per-minute rate you were promised. Mistakes abound, and by some odd coincidence, they almost always seem to favor the company!

128. **Don't forget calling cards.** If you travel, calling cards are important because they allow you to get the same rates from the road that you're used to paying at home, at least theoretically. But the big three long-distance carriers often have ridiculously high rates and fees for their cards. Before you enroll in any plan, be sure to ask about calling card rates. If the plan is otherwise perfect but the calling card rates seem too high, you can always buy low-cost prepaid cards with rates as low as five cents a minute.

129. **Save on cellular.** Cellular phones are convenient, but they can really fracture family finances. If you keep one for emergencies, consider a much less expensive pager instead. If you really need cellular, understand what you need it for before

you buy it. For example, why pay for an unlimited national calling plan if you rarely leave your state? If you don't use all the minutes that come with your monthly plan, the cost of the minutes you do use skyrockets. So think about your needs before you sign a contract. Speaking of contracts, nowadays there are many plans that don't require one. With rates and plans changing often, you're a lot better off not being locked in.

130. **Free cellular phones aren't free.** Normally you're better off getting a cheaper plan and buying your own cellular phone. Plans that include "free" phones often come with long contracts and higher monthly costs.

Education

131. **Money for nothing.** Billions of dollars of grants, scholarships, work-study programs, and low-cost loans are available every year. Don't pay a company to find them for you, because there are places you can search for free. The Internet is a great resource for this. Web sites to check out include www.fastweb.com and www.finaid.org, but there are many others. Just do a search for "college scholarships." You can also get lots of helpful advice from any college admissions office.

132. **FAFSA first.** FAFSA stands for "free application for federal student aid," and it's basically a standardized form that will help you find out what kind of aid and how much will be available to your student. Colleges and universities use it as a basis for the tuition packages they offer, and nearly every scholarship, work-study, and other dispenser of student aid also uses it. Bottom line? If you've got a kid going to college, you're going to need it, so fill it out as early as possible, especially since some grants are first come, first served. You can get

the form from any college, or you can fill it out on-line at www.fafsa.ed.gov.

133. **Beat the local bushes, too.** You can look at all the scholarship search Web sites and library books in the world and still miss college cash. Why? Because the $300 scholarship offered by your local Rotary Club isn't in there. Neither is the local Elks Club $250 essay contest or any number of other awards local civic, cultural, and religious groups may be offering in your neighborhood. Individually, the local stuff may look like small potatoes. But free money is free money: someone's got to get it; might as well be your student!

134. **Buy textbooks on-line, used, or both.** Used to be you were trapped paying outrageous prices to the monopoly known as the campus bookstore. Nowadays, thanks to the Internet, you can buy new and used textbooks on-line and save serious bucks. Do a search for "used textbooks."

Around the House

135. **Don't buy dryer softening sheets.** Instead, mix up a spray bottle with half water and half fabric softener. Spray a washcloth with the mixture and toss it in the dryer.

136. **Repaint in white.** Painting is one of the few home improvements you can make that normally adds more value to a home than it costs, assuming you do it yourself. White paint is usually cheaper, doesn't fade, makes rooms look bigger, and goes with more stuff.

137. **Clean your own carpets.** A carpet-cleaning machine is a great neighborhood co-op tool. Share the cost (maybe you can find one at a yard sale) with your neighbors, and everybody on the block saves $100 a year or more in carpet-cleaning costs.

138. **Do it yourself.** If you own a home, buy how-to books and stop calling repairmen for everything.

139. **Charge it!** Batteries, that is. Reusable batteries cost more to buy but can pay for themselves easily.

140. **Buy yesterday's technology.** One of the fundamental ways to save money is to buy yesterday's technology. A Pentium 366 computer may not play Solitaire at the speed of light, but it will probably be perfectly adequate for the tasks normal people use computers for. And it will cost a fraction of the price of the newest, fastest models. Buying the latest, greatest gadget is an expensive hobby. The same concept applies to everything from cars to bicycles to coffeemakers.

141. **Stop being so darn clean.** Americans can be obsessive when it comes to cleaning our clothes. Result? High dry-cleaning bills, high utility bills, and high clothing bills. Nobody's suggesting you should use body odor to cull your circle of friends, but the fact is that many items, especially the expensive-to-dry-clean kind, can often be worn more before we have them cleaned. Talk to haberdashers and they'll tell you that a quality men's suit should be dry-cleaned as infrequently as possible for longer life. They'd rather see you brush the suit clean than expose it to the trauma of a dry cleaner.

142. **Use inexpensive decorating techniques.** Sometimes you just need to change the look of a room. A new tablecloth can transform a dining room, and you can probably find one at the Salvation Army for $5. Plants are great decorations that you can get free by exchanging clippings with your friends. A plywood circle sitting on a round trash can looks good when you cover it with a nice tablecloth, and the base doubles as storage. Old wooden chairs and boxes look cool when they're repainted in funky colors. Bottom line? When it comes to decorating, an ounce of imagination will replace a pound of shopping!

143. **Freeze your scouring pads.** They last longer that way.

144. **Save a tree or two.** Use a clean hand towel in the kitchen instead of always reaching for paper towels.

145. **Plastic has a half-life of a million years.** Wash and reuse plastic food storage bags.

146. **Foiled again.** Aluminum foil can often be reused.

147. **Clean up on cleaners!** You can often make your own cleaners that will save money and work just as well as their heavily advertised cousins. For example, combine ½ cup of ammonia, ½ cup vinegar, and 2 tablespoons of cornstarch to a bucket of warm water and you'll have a great window cleaner. And while you're at it, use old newspaper to clean windows. Not only is it cheaper, it won't streak. *Baking soda* does the same work as carpet deodorizer, scouring powder, and toilet bowl cleaner. It can even act as an antacid and a fire extinguisher. And how about *vinegar*? Combine it with salt, and it will clean your copper pots. It also polishes chrome, removes soap scum, and cleans your coffeemaker. *Cornstarch* is more absorbent than talcum powder and pure enough to use in place of baby powder. It can also clean carpets and remove grease stains.

Pets

148. **Fido for free.** Why would anyone pay a pet store for a furry friend when there are perfectly wonderful dogs and cats for free (or nearly free) at the Humane Society? Not only are you getting an inexpensive companion, you could be saving a life! But remember before you take one home that pets can be expensive. An average-size dog can easily cost you $25 per month just in food alone.

149. **Shop your pet food.** Unless your dog and cat read or watch a lot of TV, they probably won't complain about getting generic food. Read the labels, and you'll find that name-brand pet food often has the exact ingredients at twice the price. Buying in bulk could also be a good idea, and don't forget to try on-line shopping. You might be able to save up to 50 percent at Web

sites like www.petsmart.com, www.petquarters.com, www
.planet-pets.com, or www.petmarket.com.

150. **Make your own pet toys.** Pets are like babies. They're more
likely to enjoy the box the toy came in than the toy itself.
You've got plenty of interesting, entertaining, and chewable
items lying around the house already. You can grow catnip or
find it cheap at herb stores.

151. **Use free or discounted pet services.** Odds are you're already paying taxes to subsidize some basic pet health services.
Call your local Humane Society or county facility and ask
about discounted inoculations or other services.

Babies

152. **Get stuff free!** If you have friends or neighbors that have had
babies, and don't plan to have more, help them relieve the clutter in their house by taking those outgrown items off their
hands. Think of the pleasure they'll get seeing them used again
on an even better-looking baby! (Might want to leave that out
of your sales pitch though.) And before you leave the hospital,
you'll probably also be deluged with coupons and free samples
from manufacturers hoping to hook you. Use 'em!

153. **Make your own baby food.** There are plenty of free recipes
on-line and in library books for food that is better than name
brand because it won't have as much salt, sugar, and preserva-
tives. It's also infinitely cheaper.

154. **Rent your baby clothes and supplies.** Well, not actually
rent, perhaps, but practically. Buy your baby clothes, crib,
stroller, toys, and other things at up to 75 percent off by shopping at consignment stores. When your baby outgrows them,
consign them yourself and make part of your money back. You
can even consign on-line: try www.kindercloset.com. **Big
Warning Here:** Keep in mind that some of the stuff you find

at consignment stores, yard sales, etc. might be recalled items. So beware of drawstrings on clothing (strangulation hazard) and relatively complex things like car seats and cribs. Play it safe. If in doubt, buy new.

155. **Keep abreast of the cost of formula.** You can spend $1,500 a year on formula. Breast-feeding is free and, according to many, healthier as well.

156. **Make your own bibs.** Cut the back and sleeves from an old kid's T-shirt or sweatshirt, and you're there. If you want to get fancy, stitch around the edges.

Food and Grocery

157. **Use coupons.** But only for things you'd buy anyway, not to check out new products. Organize your coupons by expiration date, and check them each time before you go to the store.

158. **Shop once a week.** Repeated trips to the grocery store cost you gas, money, and time and subject you to more impulse-buy temptations. Keep your trips to a minimum.

159. **Bend to win.** You may have never thought about the way a grocery store is laid out, but let me assure you, merchants have. Why do you think staples like milk, bread, and eggs are normally separated and/or found in the back of the store? That's so you'll have to run a gauntlet of impulse buys to reach them. And speaking of reach, more expensive items are typically displayed at eye level within easy reach. Stoop and bend to find lower cost-per-unit items.

160. **Weigh to go.** While you're in the produce section, use the handy scales to weigh preweighed bags of bulk produce. For example, if you're buying a 10-pound bag of potatoes, weigh it. Some bags will be 9½ pounds, some might be 10½. Same price. Which would you rather buy?

161. **Bring your lunch from home.** That alone can save you up to $1,000 per year.

162. **Buy in bulk.** Often warehouse stores are great places to stock up on large quantities of nonperishable items at very low prices. However, be careful not to go in to buy a sack of dog food and walk out with a new TV.

163. **Go to food stores for food and hardware stores for hardware.** Megastores that offer everything under the sun may be convenient, but you'll often pay for it. Lightbulbs are a lot cheaper at Home Depot than the grocery store.

164. **Repackage.** Put small quantities of leftover sour cream or other perishables in smaller containers. They'll last longer. Cookies, crackers, and the like will also last longer if stored in glass jars.

165. **Grate savings.** You're probably paying from one-third more to twice as much to have someone else grate your cheese for you. You'll also save by cutting up whole chickens, slicing your own pickles, slicing meat for cold cuts, and using a blender or rolling pin to make your own bread crumbs. Compare per-unit prices on items like this and you'll quickly see how much you're paying for other people's labor. (By the way, do you throw away your chicken giblets? Fry 'em up for Fido. A tail-wagging treat!)

166. **Starch savings.** Fancy boil-in-bag or flavored rices routinely cost ten times the amount of the old-fashioned kind. All it takes to make rice is the ability to boil water! Bags of smaller potatoes are often half the cost per pound of big baking potatoes. Bake two little ones instead of one big one. Your stomach won't notice.

167. **Protein savings.** The simple proteins found in beans are better for you and obviously much cheaper than the complex ones in meat, fish, and poultry. In other words, eat less meat!

168. **Pay attention.** Always compare unit pricing, always consider generic products (which often come from the same factory anyway), and always try to avoid the word *convenience*. Premade and preprocessed foods are expensive and often not as good to the taste or the body. If it's convenience you need, make your meals from scratch on Sunday and freeze them. Avoid fast food. It's horrible for you, costs a ton of money, and doesn't taste that hot anyway.

169. **Milk your budget.** Milk about to expire? Freeze it. You can thaw it out and use it later.

170. **Dialing for Domino's?** Make your own pizza. It's cheaper.

171. **Don't pop for Orville Redenbacher.** Use generic popcorn with an air popper. It's cheaper and better for you.

172. **Keep up the pressure.** Pressure cookers cook in much less time and in many cases seal in nutrients.

173. **Something cheap that's sweet to eat.** Freeze fruit juice in small paper cups and add a spoon. Instant Popsicle!

174. **Freeze your flour.** If you don't use it often, put it in a plastic bag and keep it in the freezer. While you're at it, chop up those leftover onions and put them in the freezer, too. That way they won't stink up the fridge and you'll always have chopped onions on hand. You can also freeze parsley, tomatoes, garlic, and other items that might otherwise be rotting in that vegetable drawer.

175. **Butter up the cheese.** Lightly buttering the edges of semi-hard cheese makes it less likely to form mold or dry out.

176. **Extend yourself.** Adding cottage cheese to hamburger will enhance the flavor, add protein, and allow you to increase servings from four to six per pound. And speaking of ground beef, buying that expensive extralean beef isn't necessary. As you broil your burgers, most of the fat is burned off anyway.

177. **Don't be individual.** There is almost no situation where

individual serving packages are as economical as larger containers. Buy big and divide the stuff into your own smaller storage containers.

178. **New life for old bread.** Leftover bread and rolls can be toasted in a toaster oven and chopped up into croutons.

179. **A recipe for savings.** Nobody will sue you if you alter your recipes a little. You can substitute cheaper veggies (sliced carrots) for more expensive ones (zucchini). You can probably slightly reduce the cheese or sugar in your baking without noticeably altering the taste. (Keep in mind that recipes often will "round up" ingredients to make them easier to measure.) When you read a recipe, look for ingredients that might just be included to enhance the color instead of taste and try eliminating them. There are ways of stretching just about everything. Make your cookies and muffins a bit smaller and make more of them. Add a little more water to your concentrated juice. Add extra potatoes, beans, and the like to stretch casseroles and soups.

180. **Dress for salad success.** Mix ½ cup of vinegar, 1½ teaspoons of salt, ¼ teaspoon of pepper, ½ teaspoon of dry mustard, 1 minced garlic clove, and 1 cup of olive oil. Delicious salad dressing at a fraction of the cost.

181. **Grow your own.** Next time you buy fresh garlic, save the four inner cloves. Plant them about one-half inch deep. In less than six months you'll be in garlic city! There are many other herbs and vegetables that you can grow yourself, often indoors.

182. **Don't buy water.** Paying for expensive water is further proof that enough advertising can make people do just about anything. If you really have concerns about water quality, buy one bottle of expensive water and a cheap water filter. Then you can make your own "bottled" water, pour it into your fancy bottle, look cool, and save money.

183. **You are what you eat.** Which would you rather be, an apple

or a candy bar? One of the best things about saving on food is that what's cheaper is often what's better for you. Apples cost less than candy, are more filling, and are much better for you. Water is not only healthier than soda, it's nearly free. Legumes are cheaper sources of protein than meat and better for you as well. Bottom line? Convert your junk-food junkies into fruit freaks and you'll not only save money on food, you'll save it on health care as well.

184. **Be a migrant worker.** If you live near an area that grows fruit or produce, go to a pick-it-yourself farm for bargain prices, fresh air, and a reminder of why you work in town.

185. **Be vigilant.** Bar code scanner rip-offs aren't just possible, they're common. Check your receipt before you leave the register.

186. **Creative leftovers.** Nearly every meal ends up with a few odds and ends of vegetables and/or meats. Keep two lidded plastic containers in your freezer. After every meal, put the veggie bits in one and meat bits in another. You can then periodically sprinkle the bits of meat on your pizzas or combine the two and make a great soup!

187. **Lettuce keep our lettuce longer.** Wash your lettuce thoroughly, then go outside and swing it around in a pillowcase to get rid of the excess water (and to amuse your neighbors). When you're done, put it in an airtight container or Ziploc bag and it will last at least two weeks in your refrigerator.

Travel

188. **Go off-season.** You can save 10–60 percent. In general, the best travel deals will be found if you're willing to travel when other people aren't—between November 1 to December 15, with the exception of Thanksgiving weekend.

189. **Shop around.** Airlines offer the most complicated fare

structures ever devised. But the advantage is that there are often bargains to be found if you're willing to look. The Internet can be a big help. Most major airlines now offer last-minute seat auctions, so check the Web sites of the ones that serve your city. Name-your-own-price Web sites like www.priceline .com can also save you money, as can auction Web sites like www.ebay.com or www.skyauction.com. If you travel a lot, a membership site like www.bestfares.com can quickly pay for itself with hundreds of bargains on flights, rental cars, and hotels.

190. **Hotel high jinks.** I never pay the asking price of hotels (well, unless everything in town is sold out). Hotel rooms are like highly perishable food: if they're not used that day, they're wasted. You can almost always get a better deal just by asking, but do it with a nice smile face-to-face when you check in or with friendly calls direct to the hotels you're considering. It won't work if you just call national 800 numbers, because they can't negotiate. So call area hotels and pit them against one another. ("Gee, I'd rather stay at your place, but the Holiday Inn is $20 cheaper! Can't you match their rate? Pretty please?") If nothing else, you can often get a free room upgrade just by flashing a winning smile.

191. **Get hostel.** A hostel is a budget traveler's dream, especially if you're the social type. A hostel is a cross between a dormitory and a hotel, and you can find them in most major cities in the world. Quality of accommodations vary widely, but you can often find a place to lay your head for as little as $5. Drawbacks? Sometimes you can end up in communal sleeping and bath arrangements, with boys segregated from girls. Others are more private; you have to call to find out the particulars. You can find current hostel guides at the local library, or check Internet sites like www.hostel.com.

192. **Bed-and-breakfasts.** These can sometimes save you money but almost always offer more charm and personality than ho-

tels. The more expensive the city you're visiting, the more money you're likely to save by staying at a B&B. You can find B&B guides on-line at Internet sites like www.traveldata.com and at the library.

193. **Use consolidators.** Hotel and airline consolidators can save you serious money, since they buy in bulk. You can often find them in the travel section of the Sunday paper or by doing an Internet search. Drawback? They may not offer as much flexibility in flight times or hotel locations.

194. **Fly free!** You can actually fly very inexpensively or even free if you're willing to be a courier. A courier is someone who uses his luggage allowance to transport a package for a courier company. While it may sound a bit shady, it's totally above-board, provided you're working with a reputable company. You can find one by traveling to the Internet and going to www.courier.org or www.aircourier.org. You can routinely find deals like London for $100 round-trip or Mexico City for $50. But be aware that there are major catches. For example, it's rare for two people to be able to courier together on the same flight. In addition, you'll often have a very limited time in the country you're visiting. And the best deals are last-minute ones. So courier flying is best for people who like to travel alone and are willing to fly anywhere at the drop of a hat.

195. **Use travel agents.** These guys can often get good deals, especially if you're in the market for a vacation package or cruise. When you plan a vacation, see what you can do on your own, but before you book, see if a local agent can beat the deal you found yourself.

Entertainment

196. **Use coupons to eat out.** You can probably find "entertainment" coupon books that will offer you buy-one-get-one-free

meals as well as other valuable coupons. Often the dry-cleaning coupons alone found in these books are enough to reimburse you for their $25–$30 cost. But if you buy one, make sure that you use it! You can also often find decent coupons in newspapers and city guides.

197. **Watch amateur sports.** I don't know about you, but I'd rather watch high school football, baseball, basketball, or hockey than pro any day. The seats are better, the hot dogs are cheaper, and since the athletes aren't quite as polished, the outcome of the games are less predictable and more exciting. If you do insist on pro sports, check the classifieds the week before a game. Season ticket holders unable to attend might be selling cheap.

198. **Go to happy hour.** Learn what college students nationwide have known for decades. Go to a nice lounge that offers free happy hour food, nurse a drink, and chow down!

199. **Go to local events.** Every week there is an amazing array of free or inexpensive things happening in most towns. Plays, concerts, dances, art exhibits, classes ... the list goes on and on, and you'll find it by calling your parks and recreation department or looking in your local paper or city guide. Local colleges are another place to find great low- or no-cost entertainment. See if you can get put on a few mailing lists.

200. **Lower your restaurant bills.** There are simple things you can do to dramatically lower restaurant bills. For example, have appetizers at home to somewhat satisfy your hunger and then split an entrée at the restaurant. You'll also be amazed at how much you can reduce your bill simply by skipping alcohol. Another idea is to have a romantic dinner at home, then go out for a nice dessert and coffee. Eat out during the week when you're more likely to encounter specials.

201. **Go to the library!** Why people spend so much money on books they read only once is one of life's great mysteries. Is it

because we need to fill our bookshelves with something? Anyway, if you haven't been to the library lately, you'll be amazed at just how entertaining it can be. Besides books, you'll often find videos, books on tape (great for long-distance driving), music, magazines, and Internet access (sometimes even computer software). It's normally all free because you already paid for it through your taxes. There are two other great things about libraries that bowl me over, especially when you compare them to the megabookstores. One, it seems that there's always someone friendly and helpful nearby. And two, it's never crowded!

202. **Bag the paper and magazines.** Most of us subscribe to things we don't read. If you're going to read only every third issue of that magazine, maybe you should cancel the subscription and either buy it at the newsstand when you want it or read it at the library. And nowadays, if you have Internet access, you can easily keep up with everything that's happening on the planet instantly for free. If you really love the idea of curling up with the Sunday paper, see if you can get a Sunday-only subscription.

203. **Stop upgrading your software.** If you have a computer, you might already know that software upgrading is one of the world's great rip-offs. We already have word-processing and bookkeeping programs that have bells and whistles we'll never understand, yet for some unknown reason we feel compelled to get the most recent upgrade. While it is possible that the latest and greatest version actually has a unique and timely feature, in my experience it's not likely. If what you've got ain't broke, don't pay lots of dough to upgrade it. You should also check out free or low-cost shareware at places like www.cnet.com.

204. **Don't pay for Internet access.** At least try out one of many free Internet service providers. They take only a few minutes

to set up, and you'll probably find the few annoying ads worth the $150–$250 a year you'll save. Some ideas: www.netzero .com, www.freei.net, www.altavista.com, www.bluelight.com, and freeworld.excite.com.

205. **Use your imagination.** Like so many other money-saving things, imagination is often a great substitute for currency when it comes to entertainment. When was the last time you went on a picnic? Tried out the swings at the local park? Parked your car at a scenic overlook? Went to the zoo? Went hiking? Camping? Played card or board games? There are a million ways we can entertain ourselves that involve spending little or no money. We just forgot what they were. But when you think about the most memorable and happiest times of your life, I'll bet that they didn't include paying a huge bill in a fancy restaurant or staying in an expensive hotel.

Whew! There you have it: 205 tips that will help you develop your own personal Debt Destroyer. While I did my best to make the list as complete as possible, I know it isn't. Fact is, there are thousands of ways to save money and hundreds of resources to help you do it. If you have Internet access, simply do a search for "money-saving tips." You'll be surfing the Web for weeks. Or if books are more your style, visit the library and browse the dozens of books you'll find there.

Keep in mind: The key to saving money is to do things that are painless for you. Otherwise you'll never be able to stick with it. And what's painless for you might be ridiculously hard for me, and vice versa. We've all got things that we are willing to trade our money (and therefore our lives) for. The trick is to find the ones that are really yours instead of blindly following the fake reality created for you by Madison Avenue. Reshape your reality by re-discovering what's important to you and choosing to part with your resources to experience it. Then ignore the ever-present background noise designed to keep you enslaved to debt.

KEY POINTS FROM CHAPTER 10

→ Save money by reshaping your reality and changing your attitude.

→ Don't buy anything new that you can buy used.

→ When generics are the same as name brands, use them.

→ Be vigilant and remember that every little bit helps!

→ Substitute imagination for money.

CHAPTER ELEVEN

Repairing Your Credit

At first blush, this chapter may seem as if it doesn't belong in this book. After all, if you live a life without debt, what do you care about your credit rating? Well, while I'd love to assume that everyone who reads this book is going to immediately follow its every suggestion, I know that's not going to happen. Some people may use the *Life or Debt* strategy to help reduce, but not totally erase, their debts. And that's fine. Others may follow through and eliminate all their debts, and that's even finer. Either way, your credit rating still matters.

In his book *1984*, George Orwell described a world where Big Brother was always watching. While we've managed to avoid the bleak society devoid of freedom and privacy that he described, there are components of that fictional nightmare world that we actually do deal with. Because when it comes to your credit history, Big Brother is watching!

It's almost impossible to walk through life in America without leaving footprints. We're continually giving out information about ourselves, and that information is being collected and stored in private and government computers, where it's sifted, sorted, and used to make judgments about you. Unless you're prepared to take drastic steps, you can't prevent the information from being collected. But what you can and should do is review as much of it as possible and try to shape it so it presents you accurately and in the best possible light. And one of the computerized files that warrants your close attention is your credit history, even if you intend never to borrow money again. Because your credit history could be used to make judgments about you that have nothing to do with borrowing money.

Let's talk about romance for a moment. When you first see a member of the opposite sex, you're going to notice the obvious things: Is he good-looking? Does she dress well? Does his body language suggest self-confidence? Could that sparkle in her eyes indicate a keen intellect? All these things and more initially attract us to one another. But unless we're crazy or desperate, we're not likely to jump into an intimate long-term relationship based just on a person's outward appearance. After all, Ted Bundy was a good-looking guy, but once you got to know him ... As we get a little older and wiser, we learn to look below the surface a bit to see what's really going on in there. When we go out on those first few dates, we're actually interviewing one another: we're trying to find out if what's going on inside that potential mate is as appealing as what attracted us from the outside. If the answers we get meet our expectations, then the relationship progresses and maybe becomes permanent.

Courting an employer is very similar. We show up for that initial interview just as we do for a first date: looking good and being ready to give intelligent answers to the questions we know we're going to be asked. But looking good and sounding good aren't enough for most employers. They're going to do more than talk to you. Unlike a date, they're likely to actually check your answers. They're going to go over your résumé and confirm you've done the things you've listed. They're going to call your previous employers to see what they thought of you. (Aren't you glad your dates aren't that thorough?) And it's also possible that they're going to check your credit history. That may sound unfair or irrelevant, but if you think about it, it makes perfect sense. What type of people would you rather hire (or date, for that matter), those who've demonstrated that they follow through on their promises and commitments or people who're irresponsible? Whether your credit history provides an accurate picture of these things or not, a potential employer might think it does. So many will check. Hopefully what they see when they peek under the sheets won't scare 'em away.

Another common examiner of your credit history is insurance companies, and for the same reason as your employer. These guys keep pretty sharp pencils around to figure out things like the varying degrees of risk they assume by insuring different types of people. And (surprise!) one of the things they've figured out is that people who wreck their credit are more likely to wreck their cars. That doesn't mean they won't insure you if you have an ugly credit history. But they may charge a bit more to do it. Again, this may seem irrelevant or unfair, but that's life.

So even if you never borrow money again, *it pays to make your credit history as appealing as possible*. Which means removing the blemishes you can and explaining the ones you can't.

The single most important thing that I can say about credit repair is this: *Don't ever pay anyone to fix your credit*. There are only two types of credit repair happening out there: outright rip-offs and people who charge you to do what you could do yourself for free. Do these statements look familiar? "We can remove judgments, liens, bankruptcies, and bad marks from your credit history!" "We can erase your bad credit—guaranteed!" "Create a new credit identity!" These claims all have one thing in common: They're bald-faced lies. These types of ads that show up in newspapers, tacked to telephone poles, on the radio, or on the Internet are placed by scam artists whose only goal is to separate you from your money. If you're going to fall for this stuff, you might as well try to lose thirty pounds in thirty days or make $1,000 a week from home in your spare time.

So let's set the record straight: *Nobody is going to clean up your credit overnight or give you a new credit file, no matter how much they charge.* And nobody is going to do anything for you that you can't do yourself.

Your credit rating is essentially a report card that follows you around for life. It contains lots of information about you, which you can basically boil down to four categories: personal information, credit information, public information, and inquiry information. In the personal category you'll find the usual stuff like your name, Social Security number, where you've lived, and whom you've worked for. The credit section has information on accounts you've opened, who the co-signers were, what the credit limit was, current balances, and, of course, late payments and/or delinquencies. The public information section has stuff gleaned from public records, like bankruptcy filings, tax liens, judgments, arrests, and, depending on the state you live in, child support payments. The inquiry information is simply a list of everyone who's gotten a copy of your credit report over the last two years.

Since what's in your credit report can affect you, you want to make sure all this information is accurate, and you want to do what you can to take out the dents and dings so your report is as good as it can be. So let's see how we're going to go about it.

The tool that allows you to hammer your history into the best possible shape is the Fair Credit Reporting Act (FCRA), a law that protects your privacy and establishes the rules for the collecting, reporting, and altering of information in your credit file. The companies that collect and ultimately sell all this information about you are called credit reporting agencies, or CRAs. The basic idea here is to use the FCRA with the CRAs to improve your credit report ASAP. Okay?

The first step is to take a look at the information that's in your credit report right now. Since different CRAs may keep different information, it's a good idea to check with the three biggies: Equifax, Experian, and Trans Union. You can find credit reporting agencies in the Yellow Pages under "Credit" or "Credit Reporting," but why bother when the info you need is right here:

EQUIFAX
P.O. Box 740241
Atlanta, GA 30374-0241
800-685-1111
www.equifax.com

EXPERIAN
P.O. Box 949
Allen, TX 75013-0949
888-397-3742
www.experian.com

TRANS UNION
P.O. Box 1000
Chester, PA 19022
800-916-8800
www.tuc.com

Remember, these aren't government bureaus; anyone can open a credit reporting agency, and there are lots of them. So covering these three CRAs doesn't guarantee that you'll be seeing every report on your credit history. But probably at least 90 percent of the reports ordered about you come from one of these companies, so these are the ones to focus on.

If something bad has happened to you as a result of your credit report (if, for example, you're turned down for a loan, a job, or an insurance policy), you can request a free copy of the report that caused the problem, provided you do it within sixty days of the rejection. You can also get one free credit report per year if 1) you're unemployed and plan to look for work within sixty days; 2) you're on welfare; or 3) your report is inaccurate because of fraud. Otherwise a CRA is allowed to charge you up to $8.50 for a copy of your report. That's the federal law. But there are also certain states that have passed laws that allow you to get a free copy of your credit report once every year just for the asking. They are Colorado, Georgia, Massachusetts, Maryland, New Jersey, and Vermont. (Good job, state guys! When consumers are judged by credit reports, they shouldn't have to pay for the privilege of seeing that information.)

So now that you know how to get a copy of your credit report, what are you gonna do when you get it? Well, the first thing you're going to do is stare at the report until it begins to crystallize into something legible. The reports will come with an explanation on how to read them, but these things aren't exactly in the most user-friendly format. So you'll have to go over them for a while to get a feel for how the information is presented. Once you've gotten a handle on what the report says, see if it's accurate. And don't be surprised if it isn't. A friend of mine ordered his credit report, which should have been perfect, only to find that he had a bunch of delinquencies in his credit history. The problem? His brother's credit report was mixed in with his. This type of problem, unfortunately, is far from rare. Mistakes in credit reports are very common. Depending upon the source of the statistics, from 30 percent to 90 percent of credit reports have mistakes in them.

So go over your report with a fine-tooth comb to make sure it's all true. And if it isn't? Then it's time to write a letter to the CRA to tell them to fix it. Here's an example of what you should say, pulled largely from information at the Federal Trade Commission's Web site (a great Web site, by the way; check it out at www.ftc.gov):

January 31, 2001

Sam Sample
123 Maple Street
Anytown, USA 12345

Complaint Department
Trans Union
P.O. Box 1000
Chester, PA 19022

Dear People:

I am writing to dispute the following information in my credit file. The items I dispute are also circled on the attached copy of the report I received.

The $5,000 loan from Dewey, Cheatem and Howe Finance is inaccurate because I never had a loan with this company. You must have confused my credit report with someone else's. I am requesting that this item be deleted.

The 60-day delinquency reported on Chase Manhattan Bank MasterCard account # 4567-1234-8901 is inaccurate. I never paid this bill late. I am requesting that this item be deleted.

Enclosed are copies of my canceled checks and statements that validate my claims regarding the MasterCard account. Please reinvestigate these matters and correct the disputed items as soon as possible.
Sincerely,
Sam Sample

Enclosures: canceled checks and statement copies relating to Chase Manhattan Bank MasterCard account # 4567-1234-8901

That's the basic form the letter should take. It should be sent certified mail, return receipt requested, and you should keep a copy. And while we're on the subject of dealing with credit reporting agencies, it's important that you go into this whole process with stamina and determination. Expect credit reporting agencies to drag their feet, responding slowly or not at all. Expect to have to send the same requests over and over. Expect bureaucratic quicksand and the frustration that comes with it. Because while we hope that it doesn't go that way, it often does. Credit reporting agencies get paid to compile, store, and sell your financial life story, not to clean it up. So dealing with these agencies is about as much fun as visiting the Department of Motor Vehicles on your way to the dentist. Don't think of this as a task that gets accomplished with a few pen strokes and a stamp. It's more like a long-term, excruciatingly detailed hobby. In other words, more like building a ship in a bottle than playing a video game. So deal with it when you're feeling patient and don't try to do it all at once.

Always send copies, not originals, to agencies. Always use certified mail, and get verification that it was received. If you speak to a human being, always get the full name and make a note of the conversation, including the date and time it happened. Bottom line? To get what you want from these paper pushers, get ready to organize, catalog, and push papers, too. In short, these giant CRAs are often not consumer friendly and often don't play exactly by the rules. For example, check out this section of a press release from January 2000 that I lifted from the Federal Trade Commission's Web site:

NATION'S BIG THREE CONSUMER REPORTING AGENCIES AGREE TO PAY $2.5 MILLION TO SETTLE FTC CHARGES OF VIOLATING FAIR CREDIT REPORTING ACT

Three national consumer reporting agencies, Equifax Credit Informa-tion Services, Inc. (Equifax), Trans Union LLC (Trans Union), and Exper-ian Information Solutions, Inc. (Experian), have agreed to a total of $2.5 million in payments as part of settlements negotiated by the Federal Trade Commission to resolve charges that they each violated provi-sions of the Fair Credit Reporting Act (FCRA) by failing to maintain a toll-free telephone number at which personnel are accessible to con-sumers during normal business hours. According to the FTC's com-plaints, Equifax, Trans Union and Experian (collectively, consumer reporting agencies, or CRAs) blocked millions of calls from consumers who wanted to discuss the contents and possible errors in their credit reports and kept some of those consumers on hold for unreasonably long periods of time. The proposed settlements with each CRA also would require that it meet specific performance standards to ensure that CRA personnel are accessible to consumers.

See what I mean by having to bring some patience and deter-mination to the contest? So get ready to throw your weight around if necessary. For example, suppose you write a letter to a CRA like the one preceding, requesting erroneous information be removed from your credit report. Weeks go by and you get no response. You might want to try sending the same letter, only this time add a paragraph like this:

You haven't responded to my previous request in a timely fashion, which as you should know is illegal under terms of the Fair Credit Reporting Act. Specifically, the Fair Credit Reporting Act (15 U.S.C. § 1681i) says, "If the completeness or accuracy of any item of information contained in a consumer's file at a consumer reporting agency is disputed by the consumer and the consumer notifies the agency directly of such dispute, the agency shall reinvestigate free of charge and record the current status of the disputed information, or delete the item from the file . . . before the end of the 30-day period beginning on the date on which the agency receives the notice of the dispute from the consumer." I don't know how that statement could be any clearer. Since more than 30 days have passed since my initial inquiry, I'll be expecting written confirmation that the items listed in my original dispute have been permanently removed from my credit history.

Now that you're mentally prepared for battle, let's continue. You've sent a letter to one or more CRAs describing the details of errors reflected in your credit report. The Fair Credit Reporting Act requires these agencies to investigate the items in question, unless they can determine that the request is frivolous. They normally have to do it within thirty days. What they're actually doing during this time period is forwarding information about your dispute to the company that originally reported that information to the CRA. The reporting company then has to investigate your dispute and report back to the CRA. If they indeed screwed up, it is their responsibility to notify all the other nationwide CRAs of their mistake so everyone can fix your record. And in case you didn't see it in the bit of law I quoted above, remember that the Fair Credit Reporting Act requires that disputed items that can't be verified must be removed from your file. In other words, when it comes to negative stuff in your credit file, you're innocent if they can't prove you guilty.

Let's say, for example, that you have a delinquent account that shows up on your credit history, and you know for a fact that the company that reported it has long since ceased to exist. The CRA could then have a tough time verifying that negative report, and it could therefore possibly be removed from your report. I'm not suggesting you use this tactic; I'm showing you how to remove from your credit history items that are legitimately inaccurate. Nonetheless, that's how the law reads, so in the interest of fair disclosure, I'm telling you about this potential loophole. It's kind of like pleading innocent to a speeding ticket and hoping the cop doesn't show up for the trial: you automatically get off.

In addition to removing disputed items that can't be verified, the credit reporting agencies are required to remove anything in your history that belongs in someone else's, correct any inaccurate information, complete any incomplete information, and remove duplicate information. As a common example of incomplete information, suppose your report shows late payments but doesn't reflect that the bill has now been caught up. That information has to be added. Do you have negative items that are repeated? This can happen as intercompany transfers change the account number of what is actually just one account. If information is repeated, the CRA has to remove the redundancies. So go over your report and make these CRAs conform to everything that they're required by law to do.

After the CRA is done correcting all the mistakes you've pointed out, they're required to send you a free copy of your report with the changes made. Once a disputed item has been removed, the agency can't put it back without giving you written notice and letting you know the name, address, and phone number of the company providing or verifying the information. If you request it, the CRA also has to send the corrected copy of your report to anyone who got your report in the last six months or, if the report was used for employment, during the last two years.

Suppose you dispute something in your credit report, and the CRA reinvestigates but doesn't change the negative item? Well, you can still have your statement of the dispute included in your file. Another thing you can do is send the same information about a disputed item directly to the company that originally reported it to the CRA. Then, if the company continues to report that information to CRAs, it must also include a notice that you disputed the item. And if the disputed item is wrong, the information provider can't report it ever again.

Now let's turn to the bad stuff in your credit report that's true. What do you do about that? Well, eventually negative information in your history will go away by itself, but not for a long time: seven years, unless it's a bankruptcy, in which case it's there for ten. Information about criminal convictions has no time limit. Information reported because you applied for a job with a salary of over $75,000, or applied for credit or life insurance of over $150,000, also lasts forever.

When does the seven-year clock start ticking? Generally the date when the event that caused the bad mark took place. Let's say you missed your May car payment but caught up in June. Then you stopped paying entirely, missing your July payment and every other payment after that. In September, the car finally gets repossessed. Here we have two bad items, the late May payment and the account being turned over for collection in September. The seven-year clock starts ticking on the late car payment in May. It starts ticking on the repossession in July, because that's the payment you missed, despite the fact that the car wasn't repossessed until September.

Seven years is a long time to lug around bad stuff on your credit report. Another common error is for the CRAs to continue to report expired negative items. So make sure you keep 'em honest. But here's the good news. You don't have to wait years for negative stuff to die a natural death. You can actually get rid of negative things on your credit report anytime, at least theoretically. How? Well, remember the way the system works. The CRAs are nothing more than giant computer banks, receiving information monthly from your creditors, storing it, and spitting it back out to those requesting your report. The CRAs don't create any information themselves. So if we're going to get rid of bad stuff, let's go to the people that put it there in the first place: the creditors.

There's no law that says creditors have to report delinquencies or other negatives. In fact, they don't have to report anything. The only delinquency that's required to be included in your credit history is child support. Nothing else has to be reported, and anything that has been reported can be removed at the whim of whoever provided the information in the first place. And that's the secret to fixing your credit history. As you go through this process, you may have creditors tell you that the law requires that negative items be reported on your credit history. Hogwash. They put it there, they can take it off, and there's no law against it.

Another friend of mine had a slew of negative stuff in her credit history, all the result of a time in her life when she was a lot less responsible than she is today. She's been working patiently for a number of years, off and on, to restore her credit history to pristine condition. How? She simply writes a letter to each creditor that reported a negative item and asks them to remove it. This is a particularly effective technique in either of two situations: when you're still a customer of the creditor or when you have an unpaid balance that you can negotiate with. On the next page is a letter she wrote to a credit card company that she still deals with.

Believe it or not, this simple letter, or a variation thereof, has worked for her in five instances where she's used it. So the odds of eliminating negative items placed by current creditors are pretty good. But don't think that a simple letter like this will always do the trick. Sometimes she got a response back like "I'm sorry, but we are unable to act on your request because company policy pre-

January 31, 2001

Sally Sample
123 Maple Street
Anytown, USA 12345

BankCard Services
P.O. Box 12345
Wilmington, DE 12345

Regarding: MasterCard account #1234-4567-8910

Dear People,

As you know, I have been a loyal customer of your company for more than seven years. Over that time period, I have received many offers from other companies for credit cards with lower interest rates or other terms that could have been more attractive, yet I've remained with your company.

I recently obtained a copy of my Equifax credit report and was dismayed to learn that your company has reported that I made two late payments four years ago. I'm writing today to ask you to have this negative information removed from my credit history. Having become conversant with the Fair Credit Reporting Act, I've learned that this is easily accomplished.

As you are well aware, my record of paying on time is unblemished with those two exceptions. Since even one negative item in my credit history is one too many, please repay my loyalty and responsibility by helping me have these items removed.

Thank you in advance for your timely response. I look forward to continuing our mutually beneficial relationship for many years to come.

Your pal,

Sally Sample

cludes alteration of accurate negative information." That's not a defeat; it's a challenge. If you get a response like that, do what she did: take the fight to a higher level. For example, write again, only this time to the president of the company. Maybe you can say something like "I am enclosing copies of two letters: one that I wrote asking your company for help with my credit history, and their bureaucratic response. They state in their reply that your company policy prohibits their helping me. My assumption is that your company policy also includes making a profit. I've paid you more than $2,000 in interest during the seven years I've been your loyal customer. Am I to understand that you no longer value my business enough to write one simple letter to Equifax?" Blah, blah, blah . . . you get the picture. Be a squeaky wheel for as long as it takes to get results. Remember, this is a game of patience and perseverance.

Now let's talk about negative items that show up in your credit history as a result of bills you never paid that still have balances due. Unfortunately, I can use myself as an example in this case. As you might imagine, I try to keep my credit history perfect, but when you don't pay attention, things can happen. Here's what happened to me. I took out a cell phone contract in Jacksonville, Florida, about six years ago. When I signed up, I did so with the understanding that I would be included as a part of the master contract under the television station where I appeared on the air. In other words, I would get TV station rates and could quit any-time without penalty. The sales guy said he would make that happen, but in the meantime, I'd have to sign a regular contract. That contract had lots of penalties for quitting within the first year, so naturally I was reluctant to sign it. No problem, he said, it's only a formality. Once we've verified your employment, we'll tear up this contract and you'll be golden. So I signed the restrictive contract.

About a week later, my wife got an offer to anchor a newscast in Cincinnati, so we immediately moved there. I had used my Jacksonville cell phone for about twenty minutes total. And guess what happened? You got it . . . they wanted a $300 contract termination fee. I refused to pay, we went back and forth with letters, phone calls, and so on. But finally the calls stopped, so I assumed they had finally seen the light. Wrong. Three years go by. Now it's time to buy a house, which means the mortgage lender is going to pull a copy of my credit report. Oops! What's this? A $300 uncollected account is showing up on Stacy's report. So as the mortgage approval process went into a holding pattern, I had to fix the problem fast.

Here's what I did. I called the cell phone company in Jacksonville (keeping notes of the call) and talked to the collections supervisor. In the friendliest possible way, I explained the situation, including my pending house purchase. His response, of course, was that I should pay the balance. But I said, "Tell you what . . . you can see that I have a legitimate case that your company shouldn't have billed me in the first place. But let's solve this problem and get on with our lives. I'll pay half, $150, if you'll agree to accept that as payment in full *and* remove this negative report from my credit history. If you won't remove the item, I'll pay you nothing and merely include a note in my history that this item is in dispute. I'll still get my mortgage loan, and you'll never see a penny." The supervisor readily agreed to my terms. So I asked him to send me a letter with his signature that said they'd accept $150 as payment in full and remove the negative item from my credit history. He did. Then I sent my check but restated in an accompanying letter that the check was to be deposited only on condition that it satisfied the debt in full and that the company was to immediately remove any and all negative information from my credit history. Happy ending, at least if you consider paying $150 for twenty minutes of cell time happy.

What's important here is not just that you can use unpaid balances to negotiate a better credit history. *It's crucial that you get a written agreement that it's going to occur before you pay.* Some creditors will happily tell you anything to get their money, then refuse to follow through on their promises. That's why it's so important to make notes of any phone calls, including dates, times, and names, and why it's so important to get everything in writing. Be the doctor of documentation!

What about negative items in situations where you don't have any negotiating strength? In other words, you're not a customer and you don't have an unpaid balance. Well, you can and should still write the creditors. You can build a case that you shouldn't have to suffer for years simply because you made a few mistakes, especially since you're now a new, responsible citizen. If you had problems that caused the delinquencies way back when (medical bills, lost job, and so forth), don't be shy about playing a little verbal violin music. While it's sometimes hard to believe, the readers of these letters are actual human beings just like you, albeit a bit more jaded, perhaps. So they are susceptible to the powers of persuasion, and the attempt costs only a few minutes and a stamp. If you're the militant type, you could try more intense tactics. I'm the "catch more flies with honey than vinegar" type, but if you'd rather attack your negative credit file in combat fatigues, you can write letters to creditors threatening never to do business with them again and things like that. But I'd try the mellow path first.

If all else fails, and you've got negative items that simply won't go away, you still have one option left. You can explain your negative items. This isn't nearly as good as having them removed, of course, but it's better than nothing. The law (FCRA 168i [b]) allows the consumer to include a short explanation of disputed items. Be brief; keep to one hundred words or less. What should you include? Well, think about the types of things you can dispute in your credit report: information that's inaccurate, expired, or incomplete. Any negative information that doesn't include your side of the story is definitely incomplete. So tell your side of the story!

But don't make excuses; give explanations and resolutions. For example, let's say you show one late payment on your credit card. You could say, "Payment late due to lost mail. Account brought current immediately upon being informed." Or you might say, "Defective merchandise required withholding payment. Payment made immediately upon resolution." What if you had three late payments in a row? You might say, "Late payments due to severe injury and loss of job. Accounts subsequently brought completely current." That sort of thing. Of course, I'm not suggesting you copy these sentences if they don't apply to your situation. But if you paid a bill late, there must be some explanation that you can add to soften the impact.

Okay, let's go back over the steps you're going to use to dispute negative items in your credit report. Step one: Get a copy of your credit reports from the big three CRAs. (After you get your report looking as good as possible, keep tabs on your credit history by ordering a copy from one of the big three every year.) Step two: Write to CRAs disputing every erroneous and/or negative item from every conceivable angle involving accuracy, completeness, and timeliness. Step three: Write to creditors to have negative items removed. Beg, whine, wheedle, cajole, negotiate, or do whatever's necessary to bend them to your will. Step four: For any negative items left, add a brief explanation that also provides resolution.

That's that. Your credit history is so shiny, you can see yourself! The process was kind of like hitting yourself on the head with a hammer. No fun while it was going on, but feels good when it's over!

KEY POINTS FROM CHAPTER 11

→ Your credit history can still be important, even if you never borrow money again.

→ Get a copy of your credit report and go over it thoroughly to make sure it's accurate, complete, and clear of outdated and/or duplicated information.

→ Write letters to credit bureaus to dispute negative information.

→ Write letters to creditors to get them to remove negative items.

→ Write explanations for negative items to be included with items that you can't eliminate.

CHAPTER TWELVE

Getting Help

This chapter is a special message to people who are reading this book but aren't quite ready to embark on a debt-destroying mission because their debt is already destroying them. In other words, if you've got so many bills that you're having a tough time just keeping the lights on and the landlord at bay, then now's not the time to start the *Life or Debt* program. If you suspect you may be in real trouble, first seek help to get your debts to a manageable level. Fortunately, there's plenty available, and much of it is cheap and nearby.

Open your Yellow Pages, look under "Credit and Debt Counseling," and you'll probably see lots of companies that seem to be falling all over themselves to bring you back from the brink of debt destruction. You also see them on TV and through the mail, both electronic and regular. Many of these organizations wave the nonprofit banner like a flag and tell you their services are free, or nearly free. What's the catch?

Credit counseling agencies, like most businesses, come in all types and sizes. Most get the lion's share of their income essentially by keeping a portion of the money they collect when they put you on a debt management program (DMP). When you participate in a debt management program, what's happening is that you're sending one check to the counseling agency and they're dividing it among your creditors. It's common for them to also negotiate lower interest rates and payments with your creditors. As the creditors receive their money, they give the agency a percentage of it, and that's how they keep the doors open. Historically, that percentage has been 10–12 percent, but in recent years it has declined considerably and currently hovers between 5 and 10 percent. And some creditors don't make these payments (called "fair share payments") at all. As a result, many agencies have had to start charging a small monthly fee to stay alive.

Theoretically, credit counseling agencies work kind of like Realtors when you're buying a house. You don't pay a fee, because someone else is paying it. In the case of a Realtor, the seller is paying the bill. In the case of a credit counseling agency, the lender is paying the bill. Which means that with both Realtors and credit counselors, you need to be aware of potential conflicts of interest.

Since credit counselors get paid only when they put you on a debt management program, they obviously have a powerful incentive to do so. Since these programs might well reduce your payments and interest rates, you might say, "So what?" Well, the "so what" is that a DMP could show up later as a negative item on your credit history. It may not be that big a deal (some lenders don't pay attention to this notation in your credit history at all, it probably won't lower your credit score, and it will normally drop off your report once you've successfully completed the program) but a counselor with your best interest at heart should still tell you the whole story, and this is part of the story.

Does that mean you should shun all credit counselors? Not at all. Just the opposite, in fact. If you're in such bad shape that you need one, your credit history is probably already in jeopardy, and better for a creditor to see a DMP on your credit history than several loan defaults.

But what you do need to watch for is getting hooked up with a so-called DMP mill, a company that puts virtually everybody on a debt management program simply because that's how it gets paid. If your debt dilemma includes bills that don't qualify for a DMP (like a mortgage or car loan), a DMP mill won't help you with them. You also won't get any type of budget counseling. And if your situation is so tenuous that bankruptcy should be a consideration? You'll never hear that suggestion from a DMP mill, since again, they won't make money doing that. It takes only a few minutes to sign you up for a program through a DMP mill, and if you ultimately have to file bankruptcy anyway, who cares? They collected their money for as long as you were able to stick with the program. What makes these guys even more insidious is that they can be hidden behind a nonprofit shield.

A credit counseling agency should work by helping you with all your debts and presenting you with all your options before you do anything that you can't undo. In other words, they should counsel you, not slam you into a quick fix before they've taken the time to get to know you. If you can pay your debts without going on a DMP, they should tell you. If you need to think about bankruptcy, they should tell you that.

In my experience, Consumer Credit Counseling Service is one of the best in the debt counseling industry. They've been around a long time, offer independent accreditation, counselor certification, and provide an approach as close to holistic and objective as you'll find. That's not to say there aren't other good agencies. There most certainly are. But if I'm going to suggest a nationwide option, that's the one I'd recommend. (Fair disclosure: Consumer

Credit Counseling Service sponsors my news reports in many of the cities where I'm on the air. But that's because I approached them, not the other way around. Long before they began sponsoring me, I referred viewers to them.)

In any case, no matter where you turn for help, be sure to ask some questions of the counseling agency before you agree to anything. For example, ask what percentage of clients they have on debt management programs. If the answer is nearly all, that's bad. If the answer is about half, that's good, because it shows they're trying to help their clients with other methods. Ask about fees. Ask about the amount of budget counseling you're going to get, because if you're not going to get any tools to help change the way you deal with debt, you're going to end up in the same place farther down the road. Ask if their counselors have any training and, if so, if they have any certification. Ask if the agency is accredited by an independent organization. Ask what their help will mean to your credit history. (The correct answer here is, "There's no way to tell for sure. Could even be negative. But consider the alternative." The wrong answer is, "No problem, buddy! Sign here!") The main thing to do is get a feeling for whether these people are out to help you or help themselves. If they're pushy, push your way out the door. They should be talking to you like a real counselor, not a used-car salesman.

However you choose to get help, if you can't see your way out of a debt disaster, definitely get help! And don't be ashamed or embarrassed to do so. More than a million people every year file for personal bankruptcy. Many more do nothing to try to help themselves and end up with ruined credit and lots of sleepless nights. Going to a pro for help may not be your proudest moment, but there are definitely a lot worse things that could happen. Then, when you're back on your feet, reread this book and get rid of _all_ your debts forever!

KEY POINTS FROM CHAPTER 12

➜ If you're having trouble making ends meet because of debt payments, seek out a professional debt counselor.

➜ Ask lots of questions before you sign up for any program.

➜ The shame of debt comes from ignoring it, not in seeking assistance.

CONCLUSION

Living Happy, Living Free

I've really had a riot writing this book. I hope you've enjoyed reading it, but what I hope even more is that you can use it not only to erase the debt in your life, but to wake up to a world of your own design, where you find your own version of happiness and fulfillment. Because when all is said and done, that's what life is all about.

If you want to be happy and free, then embrace the concepts you already knew before you began this book. The first is that once your basic survival needs are taken care of, *there is an inverse relationship between physical possessions and happiness*. If you're not happy, no amount of money or things is going to take you there. In fact, just the opposite is true. Happiness and physical possessions sit at opposite ends of the seesaw. Billions of dollars are being spent in advertising every year to convince us that happiness is connected to physical possessions, but it's all a lie. Accumulating "stuff" provides misery, not happiness. The more physical possessions you have, the less happy you're going to be, even if you can afford them all. Why? Because managing possessions is stressful and time-consuming, and collecting "stuff" is addictive. Once you have a physical possession, you automatically develop expectations around that possession. And the more expectations you have, the more opportunity you have for disappointment. Take cellular phones, for example. Before they were invented, you didn't have any expectation that you could talk on the phone anytime, anyplace. Now you do. So you buy a cell phone, which gives you a whole list of brand-new expectations. You expect it to work, which it frequently doesn't, and that causes you stress. You expect it to be the best available technology, which it isn't, because a week after you purchased it somebody invented digital PCS phones. You expect to pay a reasonable price for service, which you don't because of all the hidden fees and extras you're talked into buying. So to deal with the stress of not having your expectations met, you buy a new phone. But that doesn't alleviate your stress; it just starts another cycle. This is true of every physical possession you have: VCRs, TVs, telephones, cars, stereos, appliances, your house, and so forth. Each possession comes complete with its unique stress cycle, and each puts peace of mind further away. Does that mean you should never own modern conveniences? Of course not. But it does mean that you should recognize that after you've satisfied your basic physical needs for food, clothing, and shelter, everything you buy will probably make happiness harder to come by. And when you boil it down, that's simply because *your ability to be satisfied is inversely proportional to your expectations*.

Sailing is one of my favorite things to do, and it's my goal that in the not too distant future, I'll be doing it more or less full-time. I love the idea of sailing because it involves harnessing the earth's natural energy (wind) to literally move your house around the world. You can go where you want, when you want, and stay for as long as you want. Your life can be very simple while at the same time being a major adventure. You can be alone, or you can socialize with some of the most interesting people our planet has to offer.

You may think that sailing sounds stupid, but let's assume for a minute that you're hip to my drift and I've convinced you that sailing is something you also want to do. Start asking around about sailing, and one of the first things you'll hear is that sailing is very expensive. Is this true? Yes, provided you buy into the reality that boating involves basically duplicating your land-based home and putting it on the water. If that's the reality you live in, you'll have to be very rich indeed to live on a sailboat. Because having a boat big enough and fancy enough to include a washer/dryer, refrigerator/freezer, generator, TV, air conditioner, sophisticated navigation and communication equipment, and so on can cost a fortune. And once you have it, you have to pay docking fees, and then you have to pay lots of money to keep all these systems in good repair. Buying a new fifty-foot sailboat with all the bells and whistles could easily set you back $700,000, and that's just the start of your expenses. If you want to be a sailor, you could save up your entire life and never get the money together to do it. So much for that dream of freedom!

But wait a minute, because that's not the only version of reality out there. In fact, there's another way to sail. You can buy a smaller, used boat without a lot of the frills. There are many people who are sailing around the world right now in boats that cost $30,000. Boats without a freezer or generator. Even boats without an engine or the simplest radio. One of the first books I ever read on sailing was written by an English couple who have been sailing all over the world for many years without ever having had more than $20,000 at one time. They built their own boat, live very simply, and work sporadically whenever they need the money. They certainly aren't sailing in a luxury condo, but they're living their dream. They're free, and presumably they're happy. And one reason is that they ignored the apparent "reality" that confronted them when they approached sailing and instead designed their own.

Even if sailing is far from your idea of fun, there's still a lesson to be learned here. You can have what you want right now simply by redesigning your reality. You can change your expectations and never be disappointed. You can decide what makes you happy, and you can have it. The world where "the one who dies with the most toys wins" may be real, but it's not your only choice, and (in my opinion, at least) it's probably not the best use of a human life. I used to be a stockbroker, and now I'm a TV reporter (and in some broad definition, a writer, too, I guess). I used to make more money, but now I'm happier, because I'm doing what I want to do and creating value for real people instead of pushing paper around for rich people. I used to work for other people, and now I call the shots. I used to think that the only reality was Madison Avenue's version, and therefore I used to be a slave to material possessions and to debt. But now I'm free. Not because I made a ton of money and became a "success" according to the definition handed to me by corporate America, commercials, or my peers, but because I became a success according to my definition. I don't owe anybody anything, and I can live my life the way I want to. Want to join me? There are many people, just like you, who are doing it every day.

When I started doing TV news nearly fourteen years ago, I'm sure I resembled a deer in the headlights more than a genuine reporter. I never had any rehearsal or training, and there's nothing like learning your job in front of fifty thousand people! I bumbled and stumbled my way through countless reports before I did anything that remotely resembled competence. Now that I've gotten thousands of stories and live appearances under my belt, I feel much more confident about what I'm doing.

The same is true when it comes to writing a book. As with TV reporting, along with many other things in life, it's harder than it looks. So please forgive me if I'm not the world's greatest writer, but rest assured that I'll continue hammering away with other books until I get it right, or at least as right as I'm capable of getting it. If you ever want to communicate with me, you can (please try to keep death threats to a minimum, however). My consumer/personal finance Web site address is www.moneytalks.org, and my e-mail address is stacy@moneytalks.org. While I obviously can't answer every e-mail, I'd like to know if what I've chosen to do with my life is of any use in yours!

INDEX

Index

Index

Index

FAFSA (free application for federal student aid), 140–41
Fair Credit Reporting Act (FCRA), 160, 164, 165, 172
Fear-based emotions, as basis for spending, 32–36
Federal Trade Commission, 162, 164–65
Financial independence
    through debt-free living, xi–xiii, 13–14, 20, 98
    millionaire model of, 16–18
    spending habits and, 18, 19, 20
Fireplace, 135
Flour, freezing, 147
Food
    baby food, homemade, 144
    generic brands, 83, 115, 147
    protein sources, 146
    savings tips, 145–49
    shopping list, 83
    in spending plan, 72, 78, 87
    storage, 146
    wants and needs in purchase decision, 112–13, 117
401(k) plan, 56, 80
Frozen foods, 147
Furnace
    filter change, 133
    thermostat setting, 134
Furniture purchases, of prescratched furniture, 118

Gambling casinos, 56–57
Garage sales, 114, 118–19
Garlic, growing, 148
Gasoline purchases, 123
Generic brands, 48, 83, 115
Greed generation, 6–12
Groceries
    generic brands, 83, 115
    savings tips, 145–49
    shopping list, 83

    in spending plan, 72, 78, 87
    wants and needs in purchase decision, 112–13

Hamburger meat, 147
Happiness
    list, 44, 45–46
    money and, 44–45
    possessions and, 35, 43–44, 181–82
    spending for, 112–14
Health club expenses, 81–82, 120
Health insurance
    deductible, 127
    savings tips, 85, 127–28
    in spending plan, 73, 76, 87
Health maintenance organizations (HMOs), 73, 76, 78, 87, 128
Heaters, portable, 134
Heating costs, savings tips on, 133–34, 135
Heat pump, 134
Holiday sales, 117
Homes
    buying/selling tips, 132
    cleaning/maintenance tips, 141–43
    energy conservation tips, 133–36
    household inventory, 40–41
    insurance, 73, 76, 78, 87
    millionaire model of, 17
    opportunity cost of, 42
    rental, negotiating, 133
    wants and needs in purchase decision, 114
    See also Mortgage loans
Hostels, 150
Hotel rates, 150, 151
Household inventory, 40–41
Houses. *See* Homes
Humane Society, 143
Human needs, 112

Impulse buying, 57–58, 117
Income
    living beneath, 20, 36

Index

Index

Index

ABOUT THE AUTHOR

STACY JOHNSON, fascinated all his life by the power of money, has worked as an accountant, a stockbroker for E. F. Hutton, and a vice president and branch manager for Prudential Securities, advising hundreds of people on financial security. In 1991, Johnson began producing, writing, and starring in the highly successful television news series *Money Talks*.